SpringerBriefs in Computer Science

SpringerBriefs present concise summaries of cutting-edge research and practical applications across a wide spectrum of fields. Featuring compact volumes of 50 to 125 pages, the series covers a range of content from professional to academic.

Typical topics might include:

- A timely report of state-of-the art analytical techniques
- A bridge between new research results, as published in journal articles, and a contextual literature review
- A snapshot of a hot or emerging topic
- An in-depth case study or clinical example
- A presentation of core concepts that students must understand in order to make independent contributions

Briefs allow authors to present their ideas and readers to absorb them with minimal time investment. Briefs will be published as part of Springer's eBook collection, with millions of users worldwide. In addition, Briefs will be available for individual print and electronic purchase. Briefs are characterized by fast, global electronic dissemination, standard publishing contracts, easy-to-use manuscript preparation and formatting guidelines, and expedited production schedules. We aim for publication 8–12 weeks after acceptance. Both solicited and unsolicited manuscripts are considered for publication in this series.

**Indexing: This series is indexed in Scopus, Ei-Compendex, and zbMATH **

Max Smith-Creasey

Continuous Biometric Authentication Systems

An Overview

 Springer

Max Smith-Creasey
England, United Kingdom

ISSN 2191-5768 ISSN 2191-5776 (electronic)
SpringerBriefs in Computer Science
ISBN 978-3-031-49070-5 ISBN 978-3-031-49071-2 (eBook)
https://doi.org/10.1007/978-3-031-49071-2

This Springer imprint is published by the registered company Springer Nature Switzerland AG
The registered company address is: Gewerbestrasse 11, 6330 Cham, Switzerland

Paper in this product is recyclable.

About the Author

Max Smith-Creasey is a multidisciplinary data scientist and award-winning researcher. He has worked to produce technological solutions in a variety of domains, from computer security to insurance pricing. He has also conducted research in both academia and industry, with a focus on authentication solutions. Research he has conducted has resulted in publications in international conferences, articles in leading journals, and patent applications. He has spoken at a variety of technology events as a speaker and a panellist. He lives in the UK and enjoys reading and travelling. His website is www.maxsmithcreasey.com.

Acknowledgements

This book would not have been possible without the support of many friends, colleagues, and family. Thanks to Prof. M. Rajarajan for his mentorship into this topic. Many thanks to my editor for her flexibility, and everyone else at Springer that made this book possible. Thanks to the many colleagues and friends, of which there are too many to name, for the stimulating discussions on this field. Thank you to my family for providing the support, confidence, and proof-reading I have needed to complete this project. Mostly, thank you to my wife for being so selflessly supportive and effortlessly understanding during the completion of this book, and for making copious amounts of tea. This book is dedicated to you and our son.

Contents

Chapter 1
Introduction

1.1 Introduction

User computing devices are more ubiquitous than ever, engulfing our lives in the twenty-first century. Laptops allow us to access secure business networks, where we can work with sensitive files and documents. Tablet devices can be used to pay the bills, watch movies, read the news, and store many types of personal media. Smartwatches give users the capability of storing health data and receiving calls, messages, and potentially private notifications. Smartphones are usually carried with us to allow quick access to a variety of applications such as messages, banking, maps, web browsing, social media, and more. Every day we carry these (and other) devices around with us, many of which hold many times the amount of processing power that was available on 16 July 1969 to take mankind to the Moon [6].

These kinds of user devices have significant market penetration. The smartphone is a perfect example of this. It is considered the most important device for Internet access for a majority of UK users, seeing users numbering an estimated 53.58 million in 2021 (with 99% adoption in the 16–34 years old demographic) [4]. This is likely due to the increasing capabilities accessible via such user devices. This increase in device use corresponds to the average increase in time spent online which was recorded in the years 2017, 2018, 2019, and 2020 as 2 hours 57 minute, 3 hours 10 minute, 3 hours 28 minute, and 3 hours 37 minute, respectively [5]. One possibility for our obsession with some of these devices is that they offer short timescale reward cycles, which learning and behaviour research shows motivates engagement [3]. In fact, a study in the UK found 52% of users would rather use their device than simply sit and think [2].

The increase in user device adoption and use has led to these devices becoming an almost indispensable part of all aspects of our lives. Even when not around these devices, some users experience *phantom vibrations* in their pocket as if their phone had vibrated [1]. However, to fulfil the potential that a user device may offer it usually is necessary to store personal and private information on, or accessible via,

M. Smith-Creasey, *Continuous Biometric Authentication Systems*, SpringerBriefs in Computer Science, https://doi.org/10.1007/978-3-031-49071-2_1

the device. This information might include messages, photos, social media accounts, purchases, and financial data. If obtained by imposters this type of information might be used for malicious purposes, such as blackmail or identity fraud. The risk goes beyond the individual if the device also stores information private to an organisation, business, or government entity (such as intellectual property or state secrets).

These risks require that users of devices that might store personal or private data and functionalities are *authenticated*. This enables the device to verify if the user is who they claim. Traditionally, these mechanisms have been implemented (and largely still are) as knowledge-based authentication techniques (such as passwords). Such mechanisms have some well-known flaws, not least the way users often select simple passwords that they reuse on multiple systems. Recently, however, sensors on some modern devices have allowed authentication via biometrics (such as fingerprints). Though this does address some issues with knowledge-based authentication, biometric systems have also seen emerging threats such as spoof attacks.

Furthermore, the mechanisms used to authenticate devices today are often only implemented at the point-of-entry and are, therefore, known as *one-shot* authentication techniques. This means that there are no additional attempts to authenticate after the initial authentication so long as the device remains in use (otherwise it may auto lock after a time period). The consequence of this is that an attacker with access to an unlocked device can begin using it and have access to files and functionalities of the genuine user. Most traditional authentication mechanisms are also limited in that they only use one form of authentication (e.g., a single biometric). Using only one form of authentication weakens the security of the device as attackers need to only bypass one mechanism. Using only one form of authentication also comes with usability limitations such as optimum environmental conditions for facial recognition.

The traditional forms of authentication might also be seen as inconvenient. The requirement by some systems to input a form of knowledge takes time, effort, and memorisation (although minimal) from the user. Similarly, systems employing biometric authentication might require a user to place a biometric onto a sensor (e.g., a fingerprint scanner). When one considers the plethora of devices and services a user might have to use daily, it is clear that authentication can become an inconvenience (which can result in users disabling authentication altogether).

The concept of *continuous biometric authentication systems*[1] have seen considerable research interest in the last decade. These systems collect and authenticate user biometrics during normal device usage, offering security beyond the point-of-entry. This increases security in that impostors can be identified in near real-time. The ability some of these systems have shown to utilise multiple biometric traits also heightens security (as attackers would have to spoof multiple traits). The usability is

---

[1] Commonly referred to as simply *continuous authentication*, and done so in this book, but not to be confused with systems performing non-biometric machine-to-machine continuous authentication.

also increased through these systems because biometrics are collected transparently, requiring no explicit user authentication. This usability is reflected in studies in which users claimed they would use such systems. Research into continuous biometric authentication systems has been driven by recent advancements in device sensors, machine learning, and computational power. However, we authenticate in the future, it is likely that these systems will play an important role.

This book aims to bring together a wide variety of related literature to provide an overview of these continuous biometric authentication systems. The reader should come away with an understanding of the weaknesses of traditional authentication techniques and the benefits continuous authentication may provide. The reader will learn how these systems are designed, constructed, and evaluated. This book is suitable for researchers that wish to obtain an overview of the field, lecturers teaching any of the concepts covered, students that are studying the topics presented, software developers that are looking at implementing a continuous authentication system, security experts that require a knowledge of current trends, and, finally, the general reader that has an interest in cyber security.

1.2   Outline

This book begins with an insight into traditional authentication mechanisms. Then the concept, architecture, and evaluation paradigms for continuous authentication systems are discussed. Next, a summary of biometrics utilised within such systems is provided. The considerations one must keep in mind when constructing this type of system are then discussed. The book then concludes with a summary of the contents. The outline of the remainder of this book is, therefore, as follows:

Chapter 2 This chapter explores traditional user authentication. First, the three main ways to authenticate a user (namely something-you-*know*, something-you-*have*, and something-you-*are*) are introduced. These areas are then explored in detail with examples of the authentication mechanisms within each as well as a critical exploration of the limitations of each. The user perceptions of these authentication techniques are also discussed. Lastly, a summary and key takeaways are provided.

Chapter 3 This chapter introduces and describes continuous biometric authentication systems. The chapter first gives an insight into the motivations behind such systems. The concept is then defined and the key system components are described. The devices and the sensors that facilitate such systems are discussed. The datasets, user profile creation, and evaluation methodologies are then presented. The threats to such systems and the perceptions users have about them are then described. Finally, the chapter concludes by presenting a summary of the findings.

Chapter 4 In this chapter the biometrics that have been used to perform continuous authentication are detailed. First, the requirements for the selection of optimal biometrics are described. The different functionalities biometrics may be used for are then compared. The different physiological and behavioural biometrics are then described with reference to state-of-the-art systems employing them. Then systems employing multibiometric techniques and the benefits of such systems are evaluated. The key points of the chapter are then summarised to conclude the chapter.

Chapter 5 This chapter describes some practical considerations that one must consider when designing a continuous authentication system. One consideration discussed is the benefit of contextually aware systems. Next, power usage considerations are described. Then, attack mitigation considerations and techniques are described. Some relevant privacy considerations and methods are then presented. The regulatory considerations (such as some legal requirements) are also discussed. The chapter concludes by summarising the discussed considerations.

Chapter 6 This is the final chapter and concludes the book. First, the motivations for continuous authentication techniques are summarised. The main insights from the previous chapters and the relevance they have to continuous authentication going forward are discussed. Lastly, some final thoughts on continuous authentication as a future authentication technology are provided.

References

1. Deb, A.: Phantom vibration and phantom ringing among mobile phone users: a systematic review of literature. Asia-Pacif. Psychiat. **7**(3), 231–239 (2015)
2. Downtime? Half of UK smartphone owners prefer to check their devices. https://www.marketingcharts.com/digital-37529. Accessed 09 Jan 2023
3. Gazzaley, A., Rosen, L.: The Distracted Mind: Ancient Brains in a High-Tech World. MIT Press, Cambridge (2016)
4. O'Dea, S.: Smartphones in the united kingdom- statistics & facts | statista. https://www.statista.com/topics/4606/uk-smartphone-market/#topicHeader__wrapper
5. Ofcom: Online nation. https://www.ofcom.org.uk/__data/assets/pdf_file/0013/220414/online-nation-2021-report.pdf
6. Wen, C.: Chapter 8 - telemedicine, ehealth and remote care systems. In: de Fátima Marin, H., Massad, E., Gutierrez, M.A., Rodrigues, R.J., Sigulem, D. (eds.) Global Health Informatics, pp. 168–194. Academic, Cambridge (2017)

Chapter 2
Traditional Authentication

2.1 Introduction

Many users do not select optimally secure authentication options. There are many cases of reused passwords (or some variation of the password), prioritising convenience over security. Other users may select a PIN based on a date that an attacker could easily find out (such as a date of birth). However, this may be because some of the current authentication mechanisms are too cumbersome and inconvenient for many users and it leaves them selecting weaker authentication solutions. Partially, this is due to the shift in how we use technology. Before the days of smartphones, a session with a computing device may last well over an hour. Now, sessions can last seconds and are also more frequent. Some of the methods traditionally used to authenticate users lack user convenience for this new way that we use technology.

The way we authenticate ourselves on our devices has followed a similar paradigm for decades; a genuine user presents a piece of information to a computer system (some knowledge, a possession, or a biometric) that only they should be able to provide. In traditional and current computer systems, the authentication process is then complete and no subsequent authentication procedure takes place during the session. If a genuine user logs into their laptop and leaves it, an attacker could (before the system locks due to a timeout) interact with the system. Even the recent authentication technologies (such as biometric solutions) follow this traditional approach.

Whilst continuous biometric authentication schemes offer a plethora of benefits they are not yet mainstream authentication solutions. Currently, many devices (such as smartphones and laptops) still rely on more traditional authentication techniques such as passwords and one-shot biometrics to provide access. The aim of this chapter is to explore the primary authentication solutions that are currently used to authenticate users and identify the limitations of these solutions.

M. Smith-Creasey, *Continuous Biometric Authentication Systems*, SpringerBriefs in Computer Science, https://doi.org/10.1007/978-3-031-49071-2_2

2.2 User Authentication Systems

Throughout history humans have found ingenious methods of authenticating each other. Some of these methods include a shared secret (such as a spoken password), observable traits of an individual (such as their face or voice), or an object indicative of identity. Many of these historical methods of human-to-human authentication now form the basis of computer authentication techniques today (e.g., the computer password). In computing, *authentication* is commonly defined as the process that is performed to verify the identity of a user, device, or other entity in a system [65]. It should be noted that this is different to *authorisation*, which is the process of verifying if an authenticated entity is authorised to access data or functionalities.

The authentication process is tradition carried out at the point-of-entry (PoE) to a system as a prerequisite to access resources or functionality of (or via) that system. Authentication can occur between two computer systems (known as *machine-to-machine* authentication) or between a human and a system (known as *human-by-machine* authentication) [65]. Of course, the focus of this work is on the latter type of authentication which is known better as *user authentication*. User authentication is concerned with obtaining and verifying evidence that the identity of the human accessing a computer system is permitted to do so. The evidence provided for user authentication (such as a password or fingerprint) is known as an *authenticator*.

2.3 Current Mechanisms

Authentication is commonplace today. Whether a user is accessing a work laptop or their smartphone, there will often be an authentication mechanism to which they must provide evidence of their claimed identity. These mechanisms are implemented in a variety of ways. These are commonly defined as belonging to one of three different categories (sometimes called authentication *factors* [45]):

- **Something you have**: This is also known as *token-* or *possession-based* authentication. This type of authentication relies on some physical object that is in the possession of the user, such as a smartcard.
- **Something you know**: This is also known as *knowledge-based* authentication. This relies on some secret knowledge that the genuine user has and can present to a system to prove their claimed identity, such as a password.
- **Something you are**: This is also known as *biometric* authentication. This relies on the physiological (e.g., their face) or behavioural (e.g., their gait) traits of a user. Today most systems utilise physiological traits such as faces and fingerprints.

These authentication factors can be used in conjunction to form two- or three-factor authentication mechanisms (e.g., requiring a smartcard (a token) *and* a PIN (some secret knowledge)) [45]. Each authentication factor (and the mechanisms within it) has advantages and disadvantages. The American computer scientist Simson Garfinkel alluded to the disadvantages with each of these categories when he referred to them as 'something you had once, something you've forgotten, or something you once were' [4]. The following sections will describe the authentication factors, the mechanisms currently used within them, and some limitations.

2.3.1 Knowledge-Based

In the tale *Ali Baba and the Forty Thieves*, Ali Baba overhears a group of thieves saying the magic words 'open sesame' to gain access to a cave filled with stolen treasure. Cassim, Ali Baba's brother, later uses the same words to access the cave himself, intending to take as much treasure as he can, but ends up trapped when he cannot remember the words to get out. This use of secret knowledge to authenticate individuals and the risk that the knowledge is found by impostors or forgotten by users mirrors the way in which knowledge-based authentication is used today.

Knowledge-based authentication has been prominent in computing since the 1960s when the Compatible Time Sharing System (CTSS) at MIT authenticated users via passwords [101]. These techniques rely on secret knowledge that is known by the user and also known by (or can be derived by) a computer system. During the authentication process the user must provide evidence that they know this piece of knowledge. This process is often initiated at the point-of-entry to a system or resource where users will be required to manually input evidence that they know the secret knowledge. In recent years the form of this secret knowledge has primarily been a password, personal identification number (PIN), or graphical pattern.

Despite the age of knowledge-based authentication, the mechanisms remain one of the most prevalent methods of user authentication today. This is likely due to the ease of implementation; these mechanisms usually require no customised sensors or hardware [22] (as is often required for biometrics and tokens). This also means these mechanisms can often be implemented cross-device because they share common input hardware (e.g., a keyboard). Processing is often minimal because only a 1:1 comparison of the knowledge provided and the knowledge stored is required.

The strength of knowledge-based authentication systems is derived from the difficultly of an attacker to obtain, guess, or compute a user's secret knowledge. The theoretical strength of a knowledge-based authentication solution can be measured via the *entropy* (a measure uncertainty in bits) of the knowledge space. The entropy is computed for secret knowledge as $H = \log_2(K)$ where K is the number of all permutations of secret knowledge in the system [18]. As an example, 4- and 6-digit PINs will have entropies of $\log_2(10^4) \approx 13.3$ bits and $\log_2(10^6) \approx 19.9$ bits, respectfully. As entropy increases the knowledge space approaches the 'exponential wall', a point at which the exponential increase of the attempts required to crack the secret knowledge by brute force becomes infeasible for modern computing [37].

Modern systems implementing knowledge-based authentication solutions commonly enforce rules on the secret knowledge to prevent weak and guessable choices.

These rules may prohibit known words in passwords, a minimum number of steps in a graphical pattern, or common numbers such as dates in PINs. Users are also discouraged from using the same or similar secret knowledge in different systems in case of one being compromised. Other systems may require that the secret knowledge is changed periodically such that any compromised password quickly becomes obsolete before an attacker has a chance to crack or use it (though there is evidence that this might in fact lead to *less* secure passwords being used).

However, whilst the aforementioned methods are designed to maintain strong secret knowledge, they often have deleterious effects on usability. This is because the requirements of security and usability are often in conflict in knowledge-based authentication schemes [53]. The most secure forms of secret knowledge are long, random and make use of the maximum entropy, but this type of information without meaning is difficult for users to memorise. Such stringent requirements can leave users compromising security for convenience. It is common for users to base their chosen knowledge on notoriously weak but memorable traits (often relating to their personal lives) and reuse that knowledge for a variety of systems. This can lead to a non-uniform knowledge selection, resulting in a smaller distribution of secret knowledge and a smaller practical entropy than the maximum entropy [51].

Two other common attacks against knowledge-based authentication systems are *capture attacks* (in which an attacker attempts to capture the secret knowledge) and *guessing attacks* (in which an attacker attempts to guess the secret knowledge, e.g., via brute force) [51]. Capture attacks may rely on keyloggers, shoulder surfing, or social engineering. Social engineering relies on manipulating users into helping the attacker (as American technologist Bruce Schneier has noted, 'only amateurs attack machines; professionals target people' [77]). Conversely, guessing attacks involve an attacker guessing the password using techniques such as brute force or dictionary attacks. These attacks may be considered *online* at the point-of-entry or *offline* with a cryptographic hash database of the secret knowledge [51].

Knowledge-based authentication systems are not weak by nature of them using secret knowledge (e.g., the basis of encryption relies on secret knowledge in the form of cryptographic keys). Instead, the primary weakness comes from the way that secret knowledge is chosen, input, and managed by users. For such reasons it has been said that the human is the weakest link in the security chain [76]. The following sections will discuss and explore the limitations of some of the most prevalent knowledge-based authentication mechanisms, namely PINs, passwords, and patterns.

2.3.1.1 PINs

The PIN (Personal Identification Number), also known as a *numeric password* [53] or *passcode*, is a string of numeric digits, such as '1234', that is a piece of secret knowledge known by the genuine user to verify their identity. One of the earliest uses of PINs was in 1967, where they were deployed in British cash machines (originally requiring a 6-digit PIN and only changing to a 4-digit PIN when a lead engineer's wife forgot her 6-digit PIN) [13]. Since then, PINs have been used to authenticate users on a wide variety of user devices for access to many different services. This is most likely due to their simplicity to implement; requiring no specialist sensing technologies or algorithms (unlike, for example, biometrics) [53]. PINs are also quicker than some other knowledge-based authentication techniques, such as passwords, to input [58].

In 2011, Daniel Amitay, a software engineer based in the USA, released a dataset comprising a total of 204,508 user PINs that were used in an application he created for *Apple iPhone* devices.[1] This dataset has been analysed by security researchers to give insights into how users select PINs. The most used PIN was '1234' and it accounted for 4.3% of all PINs [53], meaning that there is approximately a 1 in 23 chance that guessing this PIN would provide an attacker access. In total the ten most commonly used PINs made up 15% of all PINs used. The frequency of numbers used within PINs also lack uniformity; the top three numbers used in a PIN were '1', '2', and '0' and the three least used were '8', '6', and '7' [53]. Such information can be beneficial to attackers seeking to guess PINs.

When selecting a PIN it is important to the user that it is memorable [53]. However, the less random the PIN, the greater the potential for an attacker to guess it. In [13] it was shown that (in banking) of the 23% of users that based their PIN on a date, 29% used their birth date (risky when 99% of the users carried documents with their birth date), 26% the birth date of a partner or family, and 25% an important event date. Similarly, in a survey carried out on PIN selection behaviour in [48] it was found that 26% of users selected a birth date or some other important date and 22% used a year of birth or memorable event, whereas only 11% used a random number as their PIN. The trend of users selecting dates was also found in [53] where the 50 PINs that represent the years from 1951 to 2000 represented about 5.5% of the total PINs and those likely to have been derived from a date was over 10.0%.

One of the problems with using a PIN chosen by the user for authentication is that it has been shown that users regularly choose PINs that are weak. One of the ways systems attempt to stop users selecting guessable PINs is by utilising *blacklists*. Blacklists are a database of PINs that are commonly used or often guessed and, as such, not allowed for use as they are deemed as weak by the system. Interestingly, an increase in PIN security was even found when a placebo blacklist was used which automatically denied the PIN first chosen, forcing users to rethink their initial PIN and use a PIN they believed was of greater strength [62]. However, when it was shown in [53] that 39.5% of the participants had to change their 4-digit PINs, because they were on a blacklist of the 200 most popular PINs, about 26% of users felt the new PIN was more difficult to remember. Many modern systems implement blacklists, including *Apple iOS* devices. Some blacklists for *iOS* devices that have been examined in a recent study [62] have been published online.[2]

---

[1] http://danielamitay.com/blog/2011/6/13/most-common-iphone-passcodes.

[2] https://this-pin-can-be-easily-guessed.github.io.

Some attackers may attempt a brute force attack in which they try PIN combinations until finding the correct one. Modern systems prevent this kind of attack through a technique known as *throttling* [62]. This technique restricts the time before another PIN can be input if a certain number have already been found incorrect. For example, in *iOS* the user must wait 1 minute after 5 incorrect PINs before they can try again with the throttling time increasing for each incorrect attempt (until the device is disabled after 10 incorrect guesses) [62]. The *Android OS* is more forgiving, allowing 100 guesses within around 11 hours (but only 200 guesses within around 67 days) [62]. This is worrisome considering the 100 most common PINs represented 45% of the Amitay dataset [53], therefore, giving attackers using this dataset a 45% chance of guessing the PIN within 11 hours. However, despite using throttling up to 17% of 4-digit PINs on *Android* could still be guessed within 30 hours [62].

The theoretical security of a PIN largely depends on the length of it. For example, using a 4-digit PIN provides 10,000 different options. The number of combinations can be computed by 10^l, where l is the number of digits within the PIN. Some devices allow or require more than 4-digits within a PIN today. However, 6-digits does not necessarily imply that a PIN will be secure; the most used PIN with 6-digits when a group of 332 participants were allowed to choose their own PIN was '123456' [53]. It was also found in [62] that there was minimal difference in the success rate of guessing a 4- and 6-digit PIN within the first 100 guesses. It was suggested that the reason 6-digit PINs are only marginally more secure than 4-digit PINs is because the PIN is longer and so users spent little effort on it, assuming that because of its length it is already secure. It has also been found that users find it more difficult to use 6-digit PINs than 4-digit PINs [53].

Side-channel attacks also pose a threat to PINs, in [83] it was found that the camera and microphone on a mobile device could be used to infer PINs at an accuracy of 30 and 50% with 2 and 5 attempts, respectively. Whilst 6-digit PINs are not generally more secure than a 4-digit PIN from a guessing perspective, they do have additional robustness against shoulder surfing attacks [7]. Currently, *Apple iOS* devices now require 6-digit PINs by default. It has also been suggested in recent research to combine the PIN with the behaviour of the *way* the PIN was input (i.e., via touch dynamics) to reduce successful guess attacks from 100 to 9.9% [88].

2.3.1.2 Passwords

The concept of passwords has been around for millennia, long before the invention of computers. One of the earliest accounts of passwords was in the ancient Roman military where passwords, known then as *watchwords* [30], were used to identify allies. The same concept is in William Shakespeare's *Hamlet* [82] where, in the opening scene, the sentinel Barnardo authenticates himself to Francisco by exclaiming 'Long live the King!' as he takes his position on the castle walls at Elsinore. This ancient technique to verify identity is now used on a global scale in a plethora of different computer systems. The concept relies on the genuine user

Table 2.1 The most common 50 passwords according to the UK's National Cyber Security Centre (NCSC), from their 2019 compilation of the 100,000 most common passwords [21]

Rank	Password	Rank	Password	Rank	Password	Rank	Password	Rank	Password
1	123456	11	1234567890	21	123456a	31	123abc	41	zxcvbnm
2	123456789	12	123123	22	654321	32	1q2w3e4r	42	1g2w3e4r
3	qwerty	13	000000	23	123321	33	qwe123	43	gwerty
4	password	14	iloveyou	24	666666	34	7777777	44	zag12wsx
5	111111	15	1234	25	1qaz2wsx	35	qwerty123	45	gwerty123
6	12345678	16	1q2w3e4r5t	26	myspace1	36	target123	46	555555
7	abc123	17	qwertyuiop	27	121212	37	tinkle	47	fuckyou
8	1234567	18	123	28	homelesspa	38	987654321	48	112233
9	password1	19	monkey	29	123qwe	39	qwerty1	49	asdfghjkl
10	12345	20	dragon	30	a123456	40	222222	50	1q2w3e

remembering and entering a string of characters that is secret to them into a system. If the password matches the password (or a derivation of it) stored on the system then access is granted.

The theoretical security of passwords is impressive due to the potential for many different combinations of character classes; passwords are not limited solely to numeric values as with a PIN. For example, the space for unique passwords is $62^8 = 2.2 \times 10^{14}$ for an 8-character password consisting of alphanumeric characters. However, whilst a completely random string would be the most secure password, the selection of passwords from the various character combinations and classes is not uniform [65]. As shown in Table 2.1, many users still opt for passwords that are simplistic and guessable such as dictionary words, names, and common numerical strings. Even Eric Schmidt, CEO of *Google* from 2001 to 2011, once used 'wendy!!!' (his wife's name followed by three exclamation marks) as his password [36].

It is often the case that rule-based policies are applied when passwords are created to ensure some level of strength.[3] Such rules may require that chosen passwords are of a minimum length and include special characters, capital letters, and numbers [44]. These rules aim to increase the entropy and make it more difficult for an attacker to guess a password. However, these rules are arduous, time consuming and result in passwords that are difficult to memorise [59]. In fact, most users try to avoid non-alphanumeric symbols in passwords and are more likely to write down passwords containing such symbols [44] (as they also are for passwords over 18 bits of entropy [3]). When asked for a number and a special character many users simply add the number one ('1') and exclamation mark ('!') to their passwords [91], a habit that may be exploited by attackers attempting to guess a password. It

---

[3] However, password rules are not standardised and what might be considered secure on one system may not be considered secure on another. Interestingly, e-commerce systems sometimes have lower strength password policies [32] so as not to impede usability and, therefore, profit [97].

has been suggested that the way users construct their passwords is influenced by the *endowment effect* and, therefore, have personal attachment to the way they create passwords [73].

It is also common for users to reuse passwords among different systems, making multiple systems vulnerable if one is breached. Researchers in [22] showed that in a survey of 224 participants, 51% would reuse an existing password and 26% would modify an existing password. In [68] the authors showed that in a study of 154 users, passwords were reused for 67% of their accounts and had partial reuse (containing at least a four-character string of the original password) in 79% of their accounts. One solution to password reuse is to use a *password manager*, which generates and securely stores a database of strong passwords for which can be utilised via a single strong master password (or possibly a PIN or biometric) [79].

The selection of insecure passwords can be attributed to multiple factors. One factor is the issue of memorability. The average user in [68] had an average of 26.3 accounts for which passwords were required. In [86] all study participants admitted to resetting forgotten passwords with most doing this once per month (and in doing so would reuse or adapt an existing password). Another factor is an assumption that a password is strong due to misconceptions about what makes strong passwords. In [91] it was noted that some participants felt their password secure due to the presence of an exclamation mark or the use of words that are difficult to spell.

The use of weak passwords to protect different computer systems, whether online accounts or user devices, creates an optimal environment for attackers. Tools for password cracking, such as *John the Ripper*[4] and *Hashcat*,[5] have been used to crack user passwords from leaked databases containing hashed passwords [92]. These tools may use precomputed dictionaries, rainbow tables, and even brute force techniques to crack passwords. Today users can use online services to see if their password has appeared in any recent data breach that might make it part of a dictionary attack.[6] Utilising password cracking software on GPUs (as opposed to CPUs) can, due to the large number of cores, increase the speed at which passwords can be cracked.

Passwords are also susceptible to other attacks. The input of a password into a device is a behaviour that can be observed. Therefore, shoulder surfing may be used by an attacker to watch or record the password as it is input. Social engineering has also been used to fraudulently obtain passwords by fooling users into giving them up (e.g., by phishing (or vishing) their details by posing as a legitimate system or service) [74]. Lastly, there are side channels from which a password can be obtained, one of which is via keyboard acoustic emanations of key presses [105].

Improving the theoretical entropy and usability of the password through utilising a phrase has been suggested [69] but might be vulnerable to phrase generation attacks [11]. Similarly, the NCSC recommends random words for a password (e.g.,

---

[4] https://www.openwall.com/john/.

[5] https://hashcat.net/hashcat/.

[6] https://haveibeenpwned.com offers this service.

the famous *correcthorsebatterystaple* password that appeared in the *XKCD*[7] comic), as a balance between security and usability [64]. Another method was offered in 2008 by technologist Bruce Schneier who described a scheme in which a sentence is turned into a form of mnemonic for the password, e.g., 'This little piggy went to market' could become 'tlpWENT2m' [79]. However, mnemonic-based passwords also have vulnerability to dictionary attacks (with a 400,000-sized dictionary able to crack 4% of such passwords) [55], so are also not a panacea to the password problem. However, despite the weaknesses of passwords, it remains difficult to find an authentication mechanism that fully meets the same requirements [12].

2.3.1.3 Patterns

There have been a variety of graphical authentication approaches proposed over the last few decades [10], but one of the most prominent and popular mechanisms is the graphical lock pattern. In 2011, *Google* filed a patent related to the use of patterns for authentication at the device lock screen [63]. Therefore, this mechanism has seen significant adoption on mobile devices running the *Android* operating system [89]. The popularity of the pattern can be attributed to several factors. The first is that the lock pattern is a visual unlock mechanism and psychology research has shown that humans have a good memory for visual information [85]. The second is that it has been shown to be the fastest knowledge-based authentication mechanism available on mobile devices [58] and, therefore, has the advantage of convenience for users.

In practice, the implementation of the pattern authentication mechanism consists of a simple grid of nodes, often 3×3, displayed on a touchscreen and requires the user to enter a pattern by placing their finger on a node and sequentially navigating to other nodes in the grid. Several rules commonly apply [89]. The first of which is that once a node is used within the pattern it cannot be reused. Secondly, nodes are connected via straight lines such that a node A cannot reach a node C if there is a node B in the path between nodes A and C without first connecting to node B.

The variable pattern length of 4–9 nodes provides a total of 389,112 unique pattern combinations [89]. In theory this provides an attacker a 0.00026% chance of guessing a pattern with a single attempt. However, as with most knowledge-based authentication mechanisms, the distribution of user patterns is not uniform. In fact, some pattern-usage behaviour is very predictable and can be utilised by attackers. In [89] a basic and obvious weakness was found in the starting node of a pattern; whilst each node should have a uniform 11% probability of being the starting node, the top-left corner was the starting node in 44% of cases and the centre node was the starting node in only 2% of cases. The selection of simple patterns can be attributed convenience because complex patterns consisting of more nodes, intersections, and overlaps take longer to input and increase the probability of input error [87].

---

[7] https://xkcd.com/936/.

It has been known for some time that smudge attacks (in which an attacker can see the finger smudges left on the screen after a user has unlocked a device) pose a threat to pattern unlock authentication systems [5]. There is a greater threat to smudge attacks on patterns than PINs and passwords, the latter require an attacker to construct a number or a word out of tap locations on a screen; if the digit locations were visible on the screen for a 4-digit PIN consisting of four different digits there would still be 4! = 24 different ways the PIN could be input. Patterns may be visible as a single uninterrupted path which gives two possible input variations; starting at one end or the other. This attack is reliant on a user session where there is minimal subsequent screen contact, as it may occlude or wipe the smudge pattern.

The visual element of patterns lend themselves well to memorability and, therefore, usability [87], but this is a double-edged sword because this visual element can benefit attackers observing the pattern. In [7] experiments were conducted to investigate the efficacy of shoulder surfing attacks on a variety of mobile devices. The researchers found that a pattern with six nodes on an *Android* device had a successful attack rate of 64.2% with only one observation by an attacker, rising to 79.9% with multiple observations. This has considerable poignancy when one considers that the average pattern length of users is 5.9 nodes [39]. Interestingly, however, there are few pattern unlock implementations deploying mechanisms to strengthen the pattern (e.g., via blacklists or strength meters) but it has been shown that a strength meter does encourage the selection of patterns with greater complexity [87].

In some cases, a determined attacker may even use a camera to record the genuine user input such that they can compute the expected trajectory of the pattern. An experiment demonstrating this type of attack was shown in [102]. The researchers used video footage captured at a distance of 2 m of the finger motion of the genuine user when drawing their pattern. The results show that the pattern can be reconstructed, such that over 95% of the patterns could be cracked in just five attempts. Interestingly, the study found that their attack was more successful on complex patterns compared to simple patterns. The reason for this was that, although complex patterns can reduce shoulder surfing attacks, the complex graphical structures allowed the proposed algorithms to narrow down the pattern possibilities.

Some methods have been proposed to strengthen the pattern mechanism to the discussed vulnerabilities. In [6] the authors expand the 3 × 3 grid to a 4 × 4 grid to analyse any added security benefits. Their guessing algorithm cracked 15% of 3 × 3 patterns within 20 guesses and 19% of 4 × 4 patterns within 20 guesses. The study found that many users simply expand their 3 × 3 pattern to the 4 × 4 grid. Therefore, whilst theoretically a 4 × 4 grid offers greater complexity, the selected patterns on the larger grid are still guessable. The study concluded that increasing the grid to 4 × 4 (and beyond) will not alone greatly enhance security and could hinder usability. Other methods to strengthen patterns attempt to subtly influence the user to add more diversity to their patterns when creating them [96].

2.3.2   *Possession-Based*

Possession-based authentication relies on something the user possesses. This is, therefore, a form of authentication described as being based on *something you have* [45]. The possession, often known as a *token* [25], is something that the user must have or present when using a system in order to authenticate themselves. Tokens can be based in software or in hardware [25]. Recent efforts have focused on using tokens for authenticating users in online services [81]. The concept has been around long before computers and an early implementation of such a solution can be considered the lock and key [18] (which has been in use for over 6,000 years, with one discovered in the ruins of Nineveh, the capital of ancient Assyria [27]). In this example the key is a unique physical token held by the genuine user. The key is presented to a system comprising of a lock in order to obtain access. Possession-based authentication for computer systems follows the same approach. The security of this form of authentication comes from the principle that the token contains, generates, or receives a secret and is in the possession of the genuine so that they can present to a system.

Not everything that a user can possess makes a suitable authentication token; as one might imagine there are issues of practicality, usability, and security that must be considered. Therefore, some basic properties have been proposed that authentication tokens should have. Firstly, a token must be unique so that nobody else has a copy of that token [25]. This can be achieved through basing the secret stored within the token on a random seed. Secondly, tokens must be difficult to copy such that an attacker cannot simply replicate the token (as can be done with a physical key) [25]. Thirdly, tokens must have a convenient and portable form factor (e.g., implemented on a USB flash drive or smartphone) [18]. Lastly, tokens should be cheap and easily replaceable if lost, otherwise users may be locked out of systems [18].

One of the primary advantages of using tokens to authenticate is that they may reduce the burden on the user of memorising knowledge (e.g., a password). Therefore, the secret generated by or within a token is not limited by human memory and it can have a high entropy. Of course, the disadvantage of using a token is that, as a possession, it can be taken from a user or lost. So, in practice, to increase the security of tokens and mitigate this weakness, it is common for tokens to be used as part of a multi-factor authentication process (i.e., alongside another factor of authentication such as a password or a biometric) [2]. An obvious example of this is a cash machine which requires a token (the card) *and* some knowledge (the PIN) [78].

There are different categories of tokens. The main categories are *hardware* and *software* tokens. Simply, hardware tokens take a physical form (e.g., a USB flash drive) and software (soft) tokens are facilitated via software implemented on a user's device (e.g., their smartphone) [25]. Tokens have also been categorised as *passive* or *active* [18]. Passive tokens store a static secret that is presented or communicated to a system for authentication (e.g., cards with a magnetic strip or integrated circuitry for communication of a code). The inherent weakness to passive tokens is replay attacks in which an attacker obtains the stored secret and replays it in order to spoof the genuine token (though multi-factor implementations can reduce this). Active tokens are tokens that can store a secret and generate an authentication code (or some proof of a secret) without directly presenting or communicating the secret to the system. Active tokens, if properly implemented, are not as vulnerable to replay attacks and are the dominant token for many services such as online banking [2].

Many token-based authentication solutions today implement active tokens and generate (or receive) a *one-time password* (a OTP). The security advantage of this is that because it is *one time*, an attacker would have to intercept the OTP *before* it is used and, if the OTP is a *time-based one-time password* (TOTP), usually within a small a time frame (e.g., 30 seconds). The use of OTPs mitigates replay attacks well because they change and, therefore, an attack would not be able to use the same OTP to obtain access. However, a weakness of OTP approaches is phishing attacks. If an attacker was able to fool a user into believing that a fake service was genuine then they would be able to obtain the OTP entered by the user and reuse it.

Most user devices (such as smartphones and laptops) and the services hosted on them do not use tokens as a way to authenticate, often relying more on knowledge-based and biometric-based authentication solutions. This may be due to the cost, inconvenience, or impracticality of tokens (especially hardware tokens). Tokens can be arduous for users because they can require a non-trivial user interaction (e.g., copying the OTP), which discourages broader adoption of these mechanisms [81]. Whilst tokens are not generally used alone for authenticating users on their devices they have seen use in multi-factor authentication systems (explored in Sect. 2.3.4).

2.3.2.1   Hardware-Based Tokens

Hardware-based tokens are implemented on physical hardware and come in a variety of forms. Some tokens may be small devices with an LCD display suitable of displaying a OTP. The *RSA SecurID* token is an example of this. These tokens generate a TOTP based on a secret seed shared by the token and the service, allowing the service to compute what the expected TOTP is for the user. In 2011 (when around 40 million of these tokens were in circulation) there was a breach reported on information related to the tokens, which led to RSA offering to replace customer tokens [8]. Since then, the security perception of these tokens has declined [43]. Other forms of physical tokens may include USB flash drives or smartcards (a card with an embedded microchip) [25]. Some tokens (such as smartcards) may require the system to be equipped with dedicated token-reading hardware.

There are three groups of hardware-based tokens, as described in [25]. These are *disconnected* tokens, *connected* tokens, and *contactless* tokens. Disconnected tokens have no physical or logical connection to a user device. They display some generated (e.g., a OTP) or stored authentication information that a user will need to manually input into a system to authenticate. Connected tokens are defined as those that have a physical connection to a user device such as a smartcard or a USB flash drive. They have the advantage of reducing human interaction and, therefore, minimising human error [25]. Finally, contactless tokens are those that have a logical connection to the user device but not a physical connection and, therefore, communicate some authentication knowledge wirelessly. These tokens make use of technologies such as Bluetooth, NFC, and RFID to communicate a code to the system.

The FIDO (Fast Identity Online)[8] standards have utilised tokens for authentication in online services based on public key cryptography. User registration involves the token creating a public and private key, sharing the public key with the service. Authentication involves the service sending a challenge and some metadata for the user to sign with their private key and return. The FIDO2 project is made of the W3C Web Authentication[9] (WebAuthn) standard and the FIDO Client-to-Authenticator Protocols (CTAP). The protocol CTAP2 allows for passwordless authentication through the use of external authenticator tokens such as FIDO Security Keys (e.g., a *YubiKey*[10]). These security tokens are sometimes protected with PINs and biometrics to protect their functionality. The strong advantage of the FIDO protocols is that they are strongly resistant to real-time phishing attacks because the origin domain is included in the challenge signed by the token [90]. However, the loss of an authenticator token may render a user unable to authenticate (a concern of some users [35]) and could even help an impostor to gain access to the account.

Other hardware tokens are prevalent today (often in a multi-factor authentication approach). Many users will be familiar with *Chip Authentication Program* (CAP) tokens used by banks to perform two-factor authentication (e.g., Barclays PINsentry). These tokens allow the user to input their card into a slot, enter their PIN, and perform a number of authentication functionalities (such as obtaining a OTP) [28]. This enhances security but there have been security concerns raised including potential phishing attacks [28]. In 2020, the adoption of face masks to reduce the spread of the Covid-19 virus impeded face authentication approaches on smartphones. One solution to this introduced on *Apple iPhone* devices was to authenticate only the eyes but require a token present in the form of an authenticated *Apple Watch*.[11]

Several studies have proposed token-based solutions for authenticating modern devices. In [54] the authors propose a Bluetooth-connected token to authenticate the user and can easily be implemented on current smartphones. They showed that the solution implemented with an Android smartphone and an MSP430-based microcontroller authenticated a user in under a second without the need for additional user action. However, the downside of hardware-based tokens is that they incur a cost to provide and they also inconvenience users by requiring them to remember to carry a physical token. This can be arduous for users [81] and may be even worse for users that must carry multiple tokens on their person [2].

---

[8] https://fidoalliance.org/.

[9] https://www.w3.org/TR/webauthn/.

[10] https://www.yubico.com.

[11] https://support.apple.com/en-gb/HT212208.

Furthermore, using hardware-based tokens for user devices would need a token to be provided alongside the user device. Therefore, the use of such tokens to authenticate a user device (or a service on that device) is often used for specific and specialist reasons.

2.3.2.2   Software-Based Tokens

A software token (commonly known as a *soft token*) is a token that relies on a software component present on a user device, such as an application for storing, receiving, or generating an authentication code [25]. Since soft tokens are stored on user devices, they do not require a separate piece of dedicated hardware. This improves the convenience of soft tokens over hardware-based tokens because they rely on a device the user already owns and is usually on their person (often a mobile device [43]). Software tokens can be stored on general-purpose electronic devices including desktop computers, laptops, tablets, or smartphones [25]. However, this installation of soft tokens on general-purpose devices may carry a security risk if the device becomes compromised through malware. Furthermore, soft tokens may be able to be copied or accessed between devices depending on the implementation (e.g., a OTP sent to an application installed on multiple devices) [25].

Soft tokens have several implementations that modern users will be familiar with. One simple method that is considered a form of soft token implementation is the delivery of an SMS to a user's mobile phone [24]. This approach relies on software already on the phone and, therefore, does not require any dedicated application to be installed. Often the delivered SMS is a OTP computed and sent by a service (e.g., 6-digits) supporting a two-factor authentication mechanism. This implementation supports a large audience because SMS messaging is a ubiquitous functionality of mobile phones, usually requires no additional software installation, and is low cost to implement [43]. However, the device must have a mobile network signal in order to receive the OTP, which cannot always be guaranteed.

More recent soft tokens include *Google Authenticator*, which facilitates a two-factor authentication process via the generation of a OTP. Such applications generate a OTP based on secret user key and some other factors. During registration the service generates a secret user key, which is usually displayed as a QR code that can be scanned to enrol the key [43]. Once the key is enrolled the application supports both the HMAC-based OTP (HOTP)[12] algorithm and the Time-based OTP (TOTP)[13] algorithm. The HOTP algorithm provides a OTP from an extract of the hash (SHA-1 by default) of the secret key and an incremental counter. The TOTP algorithm is an extension of the HOTP algorithm and provides a OTP from an extract of the hash of the secret key and the time. When the user authenticates with the generated OTP, the service performs the same algorithm to compare them. The

---

[12] https://datatracker.ietf.org/doc/html/rfc4226.

[13] https://datatracker.ietf.org/doc/html/rfc6238.

benefit of this application is that it requires no internet connection or mobile signal. Code for an earlier version of *Google Authenticator* is available online.[14]

2.3.3 Biometric-Based

We have known for many years that our bodily characteristics have many identifying traits. In the 1870s, a system proposed by Alphonse Bertillon captured body measurements (e.g., skull diameter, arm length, and foot length) to identify prisoners [98]. In 1912, India's government required passports to include a descriptive roll of such traits, including height, eye colour, hair colour and 'any distinctive marks' (as well as a fingerprint in lieu of a signature if one could not be provided) [84]. In 1915, the UK government required passports to contain even more characteristics, including information about the forehead, nose, mouth, chin, and 'any special peculiarities' [84]. Today these human measurements are known to us as biometrics (a term used since circa 1980 [47]) and classified as an authentication mechanism based on something the user *is* [81]. The term *biometrics* comes from Ancient Greek, with 'bios' meaning 'life' and 'metros' meaning 'to measure' [57]. The study of biometrics is, therefore, in essence, the study of human measurements. As shown, the concept is not new and in one form or another biometrics has been a focus of study for well over 100 years (with some notable interest from law enforcement).

Biometrics are abundant within our day-to-day lives and see wide-ranging and successful use cases. In 2009, the Indian government launched *Aadhaar*, a system in which citizens are provided a 12-digit national identity number and enrolled via ten fingerprints, two iris scans, and a face photograph.[15] The Aadhaar system shows biometrics implemented at scale and has, to date, enrolled more than 1.3 billion profiles and performed more than 71 billion authentications.[16] Today many modern smartphones, tablets, and laptops also offer the option to authenticate the user via biometrics (often via a face or fingerprint). It is also common to see customer service lines (e.g., for banking) perform voice recognition to verify user identity. The ability to authenticate users accurately via biometrics has been advanced in recent years by, among other factors, improvements in machine learning (e.g., via neural networks), processing power, and sensing technologies. The inclusion of biometrics within modern life appears set to continue, with the global biometrics market forecast to reach $82.8 billion by 2027, from an estimated $24.1 billion in 2020.[17]

A biometric-based authentication system will capture biometric information either related to a user's physiology (such as fingerprint, face, or retina) or their

---

[14] https://github.com/google/google-authenticator.

[15] https://uidai.gov.in/what-is-aadhaar.html.

[16] https://uidai.gov.in/aadhaar_dashboard/index.php.

[17] https://www.biometricupdate.com/202010/global-biometrics-market-forecast-to-surpass-82b-by-2027-despite-pandemic.

behaviour (such as voice, gait, or keystroke dynamics) [47]. This requires a sensor module to enable the biometric to be captured (e.g., a camera for face capture) [47]. Firstly, before the user can be authenticated, it is necessary for the genuine user to enrol their biometric information within the system. The biometric (often represented as a set of salient features computed by a feature extraction module [46]) is enrolled in a storage module (sometimes within a secure enclave on modern devices) such that future biometric samples can be compared to it. After enrolment the system can capture, process, and authenticate biometrics via a matching module that compares them to the enrolled biometrics to decide if they sufficiently match.

Unlike the previous two forms of authentication (knowledge- and possession-based authentication), which require an identical authenticator match, it is difficult for biometric data to identically match the biometrics first enrolled [18]. The difficulty in identically matching biometrics is due to a number of reasons, including variation in the way a biometric is presented to a sensor (e.g., difference in finger placement for fingerprints) and subtle changes in the biometric (e.g., hair growth for faces). This results in most biometric systems providing a match *score* rather than a Boolean match or no-match decision. When matching biometric data it is, therefore, common to utilise a threshold [2]. Scores over the threshold denote a match and scores under the threshold denote no-match. The threshold selection can be seen as selecting a trade-off between security and usability, explored further in Sect. 3.6.1.

Utilising biometrics for authentication purposes carries a variety of advantages [47]. One advantage of biometrics over knowledge- and possession-based authentication systems is that it is information always with the user (inherent to their physiology and behaviour) and, therefore, does not suffer from the issue of being forgotten or lost. Furthermore, biometrics do not suffer from weaknesses arising due to human factors that commonly see users select weak passwords [81]. The use of biometrics is also often faster than entering a PIN or a password and, given that users may authenticate many times a day, may save a full day of time over several years [33]. Biometric authentication systems can also have the advantage of enhancing system integrity through non-repudiation and can detect multiple enrolments via negative recognition (e.g., preventing 'double dipping' in welfare systems) [47].

Whilst biometrics are a secure and usable form of modern authentication there are some caveats. There are a variety of attacks that may be performed on biometric authentication systems, not least of which is the *presentation attack*. The presentation attacks present some artifact (such as a spoof of the genuine user's face) to the input sensor to interfere with normal system operation (usually to gain improper access). Current implementations of biometric authentication also often rely only on a single biometric, meaning attacker must only successfully spoof one biometric to gain access. There is also the requirement for a *fallback* authentication mechanism because there is the possibility of falsely rejecting the genuine user. The fallback mechanism can weaken the authentication process if (as is sometimes the case) the fallback is weaker than the biometric [93]. Finally, current systems deploy biometrics only at the point-of-entry and do not tend to re-authenticate beyond that point.

2.3.3.1 Face

Systems for obtaining facial measurements were proposed as early as 1888 in work published by Sir Francis Galton [34]. However, it was not until the 1960s that research into automated face recognition began [56]. Techniques to detect and recognise faces started off slowly, though in recent years significant progress has been made. Much of this progress has been fuelled by the success of modern machine learning techniques, namely convolutional neural networks (CNNs), in detecting and recognising faces [4]. The ability to recognise faces comes naturally to humans and is present even in newborn infants, who show a preference for the face of their mother [66]. The ability of humans to recognise faces is largely consistent as we age, even in changes in lighting, viewing angle, and distance [70] (situations that computers can sometimes struggle with [75]). The work to replicate this in computing now sees many modern user devices successfully protected via face-based authentication mechanisms.

Systems authenticating faces generally carry out a process of capturing data (e.g., from a camera), detecting a face, then (usually after pre-processing and feature extraction) matching that face to a stored template [47]. Many devices and services have recently sought to include the option to authenticate via the face. One reason for this is that, unlike with fingerprint scanners, most devices now already come equipped with a camera [99]. However, there are attacks on such systems that see attackers obtain the genuine face (trivial in the days of social media) and present a spoof of it (e.g., a print out) to the camera. Methods to mitigate such attacks have been investigated. Some of these systems rely on differences in the colour, reflection, blur, and texture that are obtained from live faces and spoofed faces [67]. Other mitigation attempts use motion analysis and build on the fact that humans blink every 2–4 seconds [1], though attackers might attempt to bypass this with a video.

In 2011 the fourth major version of *Android*, called *Ice Cream Sandwich*, was released. Included in the new features was *Face Unlock*, a face authentication mechanism that would (if the user desired) take the place of the knowledge-based device unlock mechanism. However, in [26] the authors found that, in a study of 383 users, 38.5% of those that had Face Unlock on their devices had deactivated it with 36% citing usability issues and 29% citing reliability issues. The early implementations of Face Unlock were also reported to be susceptible to spoof attacks, in which a photograph of the genuine face could unlock the device.[18] Since the release of Face Unlock, such authentication mechanisms on smartphones have generally improved and become faster, more accurate, and more robust to spoof attacks.

However, spoof attacks still remain a problem on some smartphone devices and even in 2019 it was reported that of 110 smartphones tested 42 were susceptible

---

[18] https://www.wired.com/2011/11/video-ice-cream-sandwich-face-unlock-defeated-with-photo/.

to spoof attacks using a simple photo of the genuine user.[19] Other attacks include taking the smartphone of a user and presenting to the camera the live face of the genuine user without their knowledge (e.g., whilst they are asleep). It was reported by the BBC in 2019 that such an attack was possible with Face Unlock on the *Google Pixel 4*, because it could unlock the device even if the user's eyes were closed.[20] To mitigate this, some systems now require that a user's eyes are open and that the user's attention is detected.[21] Another issue of most camera-based authentication mechanisms is that they are susceptible to pose, illumination, and activity variations that can make recognition difficult [18]. This is reflected in [9], where Face Unlock was found to be the most difficult authentication mechanism to use in dark environments.

In 2015, *Windows Hello* allowed owners of devices running Windows 10 to authenticate using their face. The face authentication mechanism uses a camera configured for near infrared (NIR) imaging to capture the face in various illumination conditions. The system forms a feature histogram representing the light and dark differences around specific points that it can compare to the enrolled face [14]. The false acceptance rate reported for this is 0.001% with a false rejection rate of less than 5% (indicating a preference has been given to security over usability).[22] However, in 2018 it was reported that versions of the system have previously been shown to be spoofed by a printed NIR face image of the genuine user.[23]

Thus far the discussed authentication mechanisms that currently authenticate via faces do so using 2D techniques. In 2017, *Apple* launched the *iPhone X* with a new 3D face recognition mechanism coined *FaceID* [14]. The device projects more than 30,000 infrared dots onto the user's face and uses an infrared camera to capture the subsequent pattern. The distance between the dots allows for a depth map of the face to be constructed. This automatically makes spoofing difficult as it rules out the ability for simpler 2D attacks to fool the system [33]. The chance of a random person being able to gain access to a device protected with FaceID is 1 in 1,000,000 [33], making it as secure as a 6-digit PIN (assuming uniform PIN selection). There have been reports, however, that devices may be able to be unlocked by the face of closely related individuals (e.g., twins) [4] and Apple has stated the probability of a false match is different for twins and siblings who look like the user and for children under the age of 13 (because their distinct facial features may not have fully

---

[19] https://www.zdnet.com/article/facial-recognition-doesnt-work-as-intended-on-42-of-110-tested-smartphones/.

[20] https://www.bbc.co.uk/news/technology-50085630.

[21] https://support.apple.com/en-gb/HT208108.

[22] https://docs.microsoft.com/en-us/windows-hardware/design/device-experiences/windows-hello-face-authentication.

[23] https://nakedsecurity.sophos.com/2018/01/02/windows-hello-face-recognition-spoofed-with-photographs/.

developed).[24] Other 3D face authentication systems might utilise acoustic sensing [104].

2.3.3.2   Fingerprint

Humans throughout history have known that their fingerprints have unique characteristics and have long used them to signature their items and art [60]. One of the first systematic uses of fingerprints was in 1858 when Sir William Herschel, a British civil servant working in India, introduced the use of fingerprints (and handprints) to sign contracts [41]. In the 1870s, Henry Faulds, a Scottish doctor and missionary, noticed fingerprints on ancient Japanese pottery and wrote to Charles Darwin about the use of fingerprints for identification [98]. Darwin subsequently motivated Francis Galton, his cousin, to investigate fingerprints and in 1888 Galton wrote about identification via the 'spirals and whorls' of fingerprints [34]. Sir Edward Henry, Commissioner of the Metropolitan Police of London from 1903 to 1918, built on this in 1900 and published a book describing the classification of fingerprints based on their unique characteristics [40]. More than 100 years later fingerprints are one still of the most widely used and accurate ways to authenticate [60].

The uniqueness of fingerprints comes from the different patterns of ridges and valleys contained within them for different individuals (determined during the first seven months of foetal development) [47]. These ridges on the skin are composed of two layers, the inner dermis and the outer epidermis where the ridges emerge [47]. The fingerprints are so persistent that they can return even after superficial damage to the epidermis [47]. Utilising these ridge characteristics is done by feature-based means at multiple levels [60]. Level 1 represents a ridge orientation map, level 2 represents ridge characteristics (such as beginnings, endings, merges, etc.) and are known as minutiae,[25] level 3 represents the inner pores and outer contours of the edges [60]. The fingerprint image can be obtained via sensors utilising capacitive, ultrasonic, capacitive, and piezoelectric technologies. Capacitance sensors are most commonly used in laptops, tablets, and smartphones today (including in *Apple's TouchID*) because they are very small in size and easily embedded [47].

The accuracy and speed of fingerprints have seen them become a standard authentication mechanism on a variety of devices (and for services on those devices). In 2013 *Apple* released the *iPhone 5S* including *TouchID*, a fingerprint authentication mechanism. The chance of an impostor fingerprint unlocking the device is 1 in 50,000, making it theoretically more secure than a 4-digit PIN but less secure than a 6-digit PIN (assuming uniform selection of PINs) [33]. However, days after the release, Germany's *Chaos Computer Club* managed to bypass the system by lifting a fingerprint of the genuine user off a glass surface and then making a

---

[24] https://support.apple.com/en-gb/HT208108.

[25] Coming from 'minutia', meaning 'small detail'.

spoof fingerprint.[26] In 2014 the same group managed to spoof the fingerprint of the then German Defence Minister, Ursula von der Leyen, using only a picture of the minister that contained her fingerprints.[27] Of course, the immutability benefit of fingerprints is also the drawback; a stolen fingerprint cannot be changed and if an attacker obtains a fingerprint of a user (e.g., via their smartphone screen) they may be able to spoof it and gain access to any device or service that uses that fingerprint.

Spoof attacks remain one of the biggest threats to fingerprint scanners and many attacks have been proposed. In [15] a simple 2D spoofing method consisting of a fingerprint printout was shown to bypass fingerprint scanners on smartphones. Approaches creating 3D fingerprints from materials, such as gelatine and silicone, have also been utilised to generate fingerprint spoofs [61]. The field of liveness detection offers some mitigation to fingerprint spoofing [61]. The use of fingerprints to authenticate user devices and services has provided attackers with a new vector through which to break into systems. Liveness detection techniques may be hardware-based (e.g., sensors for blood flow detection) or software-based (e.g., processing the image for pore detection) [17]. However, the battle between those trying to spoof fingerprints and those trying to protect fingerprint systems is always ongoing.

Other weaknesses may arise due to implementation. In 2019 it was found that the ultrasonic fingerprint sensor (implemented under the surface of the touchscreen) could potentially be unlocked by anybody.[28] This was found to be an issue that came about due to a £2.70 ($3.80) gel screen protector which confused the sensor into effectively registering the screen protector as the fingerprint. In some systems it may even be possible for an attacker to bypass the fingerprint scanner altogether by making use of a backup authentication mechanism. On many devices implementing biometrics, the option to default to a PIN, password, or pattern exists. Forcing a system to fallback to a different form of authentication that may be easier for attackers to bypass is a well-known attack vector [71].

2.3.3.3 Voice

It is said in The Old Testament (Book of Judges (12:5–6)) that the Gileadites would identify enemy Ephraimites at the fords of the Jordan by making them say the word 'Shibboleth'. Those from Ephraim could not pronounce this and would instead say 'Sibboleth', at which point the men of Gilead would seize and kill them. Humans are innately well-equipped to recognise different voices, but replicating this behaviour in computer systems has seen decades of research. Since the early

---

[26] https://www.theguardian.com/technology/2013/sep/22/apple-iphone-fingerprint-scanner-hacked.

[27] https://www.theguardian.com/technology/2014/dec/30/hacker-fakes-german-ministers-fingerprints-using-photos-of-her-hands.

[28] https://www.bbc.co.uk/news/technology-50080586.

1960s, there have been efforts to produce automated speaker verification systems via investigating pattern recognition and feature extraction techniques [98]. This is because the voice contains physiological and behavioural characteristics that have sufficient distinctiveness between individuals to allow them to be differentiated.

Voice biometrics can feasibly be captured to authenticate users on any device that contains a microphone. However, the nature of utilising voice to authenticate users may be impractical to do in certain situations. This may be due to rules about noise in the local environment restricting the user from speaking to authenticate (e.g., in a library). There is also the issue of the quality of the voice collection due to the possible presence of environmental noise [18]. This is possibly why many user devices do not rely on voice biometrics to explicitly authenticate users at the point-of-entry. The use of voice biometrics to authenticate today is generally applied to specific use cases in which it is likely that the user will use their voice.

One of the primary use cases for voice biometrics is authenticating customers over a telephone call. In recent years it has become common to utilise a user's voice to replace (or supplement) some knowledge-based authentication mechanism. This is a practice that has been adopted by several prominent banks in the UK and requires that a user enrol and authenticate their voice via a phrase often including 'my voice is my password' [94]. However, these systems have not been implemented without issue. In 2017 a reporter set up an account with a major bank and opted to use the voice authentication service. When the reporter's non-identical twin brother mimicked his voice he was authenticated and granted access to the account. This is an issue of siblings having generally similar voices (due to closeness in physiology and in behaviours such as accent). It was also reported that the system allowed attempts to authenticate after an attacker's voice had already failed on 20 separate occasions spread over 12 minutes, indicating it was not subject to the same limitations on attempts as fingerprints or faces on smartphones.

Advances in natural language processing have led to voice-controlled virtual assistants becoming commonplace in our lives today with Apple's Siri (2010), Microsoft's Cortana (2013), Amazon's Echo (2014), and Google's Assistant (2016) dominating the market. Interacting with these assistants is done via a range of user devices including dedicated smart speakers, smartwatches, smartphones, tablets, and laptops. Initially, whilst virtual assistants would respond to voice commands, it was uncommon for them to authenticate the voice. This led to reports of attackers standing outside a house and speaking loudly to Siri on an iPad inside to unlock the front door or making unauthorised purchases via Alexa voice commands [42]. Efforts have now been made to mitigate this abuse of virtual assistants and seen many adopt voice authentication, wherein the assistant will not fulfil certain functionalities if it does not recognise the voice. More developed attacks, such as *DolphinAttack* [103], may utilise inaudible ultrasonic voice commands to control virtual assistants.

Some systems mitigate replay attacks by requesting a user speaks a set of numbers or words that the system has not recorded for the user. This offers a level of protection against attackers that have obtained a recording of the authentication phrase (because it would be different for each authentication attempt). However, there are several limitations to this strategy. Firstly, if the attacker had enough of the user's voice (e.g., if they obtained voice clips from a podcast) it is feasible they could construct new sentences made from clips of the genuine user. Secondly, a recent trend of deep fakes has led to text-to-speech systems in which an attacker can utilise as little as 5 seconds of the genuine voice alongside a new sentence to obtain audio of the sentence in the voice of the user [49]. Whilst such fakes are at an early stage they have already been shown to bypass Microsoft's voice API at Black Hat 2018.[29]

2.3.4 Multi-factor

The concepts of knowledge-based, possession-based, and biometric-based authentication have each been covered individually, but two or more can also be used in conjunction with one another in an approach known as *multi-factor* authentication. Multi-factor authentication is already a part of everyday life. Every time we use a cash machine and provide our bank card and PIN we are using a form of multi-factor authentication known as *two-factor* authentication, the card is a possession and the PIN is a piece of knowledge. When we log in to online services with a username and password some services will send an SMS message to our mobile phone such that we can also be verified via a soft token as a second factor. Multi-factor authentication increases the security of a system as an attacker would need to have stolen or spoofed multiple factors to gain access to the system. Attackers that have obtained access to a user's password can do little with it if the system also requires another factor (e.g., a token or a biometric) that they do not have.

There has been a shift toward multi-factor authentication in industry, partially motivated by the millions of records exposed by hackers every day alongside identity fraud becoming one of the fastest growing crimes in recent years [24]. In utilising multi-factor authentication additional layers of security are added to strengthen the authentication strategy. Multi-factor authentication can also hold strong non-repudiation properties [24]. If a user were to log in to a system with a username and password, it may be plausible that the credentials were stolen, it would be less plausible that a fingerprint or user possession was also stolen. Therefore, it can be asserted with greater evidence that the genuine user accessed the system. Most practical multi-factor authentication solutions are two-factor approaches, though *three-factor* solutions have also been researched [52].

Despite the security advantages that multi-factor authentication can bring to a system, it can come with the disadvantage of increasing complexity and, therefore, authentication time. For example, users that are required to utilise a soft token in addition to a password must spend additional time and effort over those that do not. Researchers in [29] survey the real-world use of 4,275 students, faculty, and

---

[29] https://threatpost.com/black-hat-2018-voice-authentication-is-broken-researchers-say/134926/.

staff at Brigham Young University to measure user sentiment toward *Duo* two-factor authentication. More than half of the participants felt that the two-factor authentication did increase security. However, more than 80% found it 'annoying', and almost 70% found that it takes too much time. Consequently, it was found that around 50% of the participants would prefer not to use the two-factor authentication.

2.3.5   Other

Whilst it is generally observed within the literature that there are three primary ways a user can authenticate, there have been other works that discuss other factors for authentication. One of the most popular of these is *someplace you are* [52]. This form of authentication may relate to where a user is located and whether that location is trusted according to a policy. This would likely make use of Global Positioning System (GPS) functionality (available on most smartphones), though might also use Internet Protocol (IP) addresses. However, this particular authentication factor may be vulnerable to spoofing if an attacker can work out the trusted locations. Another factor might be *sometime you access* a computer system [24]. This factor might be used to authenticate users based on their regular access times or on regular business office hours (e.g., 9AM–5PM). Though this factor might also be at risk from attackers that observe the specific times that access is permitted to the system.

2.4   User Perceptions

The user perceptions of traditional authentication approaches are important to consider because they can help refine future authentication systems. Many studies indicate that user perception of common authentication approaches is negative due to inconvenience. This can lead users to opt for weaker, but easier, authentication approaches that prioritise convenience. Rarer perceptions on authentication may come from religious beliefs; some Christian groups consider biometrics a 'Mark of the Beast' based on language in the New Testament's Book of Revelation [80]. Sometimes a user's incorrect perception of what makes robust security can inadvertently weaken authenticators, such as many users falsely believing certain phrases or keyboard patterns are more random than they actually are.

   Researchers in [58] analysed the nuances of unlocking *Android* smartphones with knowledge-based authentication. The study monitored the devices of 41 volunteers for 20 days collecting statistics on PIN, password, and pattern mechanisms. Only 53.7% of the users used any authentication mechanism; 4.8% used alphanumeric passwords, 12.2% used PINs, and 36.6% used a pattern. Devices were unlocked 46 times a day on average and patterns were the fastest form of authentication at 1.7 seconds but had a higher input error rate than PINs. The authors in [95] also found a higher input error rate with patterns than PINs but found patterns rated higher in terms of ease-of-use, quality of feedback, and likeability. These studies indicate that users may perceive factors such as ease-of-use and reduction in entry time (as with patterns) as more important than a lower input error rate (as with PINs).

Some studies show that user perception of knowledge-based authentication on mobile devices is so poor that significant percentages of users opt for no authentication mechanism at all. The authors in [31] found 40% of 2,518 users did not use any authentication with inconvenience indicated as the primary reason for this. A study analysing risk perception and unlocking behaviour found 57.1% of users had no form of authentication with the majority reasoning that it was inconvenient and unnecessary [38]. The inconvenience can be understood as they found some users spent up to 9% of all interactions authenticating. This is likely due to short-burst sessions [50]. Another recent study [72] of 500 users found that 25.4% of users had no authentication and many found authentication inconvenient. This lack of authentication on mobile devices is surprising given that users are more concerned about privacy on their mobile devices in comparison to their laptops [16].

The use of biometrics is often perceived as more convenient than knowledge-based mechanisms [100]. Studies indicate users see biometrics as an acceptable factor for authentication (83% of users considered them acceptable in early smart-phones [19]). This is further evidenced by the number of user devices today that allow for some form of biometric authentication (e.g., via fingerprints and faces). However, there is an understandable perception regarding the storage of the biometrics, with a majority of users in one study preferring they were kept on the device (rather than sent to a remote server) [106]. Another study found only 35% of users favoured network storage over device storage [19]. Similarly, in another study participants reported they would be uncomfortable with biometrics leaving the device [20].

The possession factor is distinct from utilising biometric or knowledge-based factors in that it is the only factor that requires a physical object present acting as or storing a token. The obvious issue here is that a possession can quite easily be lost or stolen. This can hinder the convenience of possession-based factors [2], which might subsequently lead to poor user perception and adoption. Some works have tried to improve on the usability of a possession (specifically the FIDO Security Key) as a second factor, though still found that users did not perceive the benefits of the approach beyond using their passwords alone [23].

2.5 Summary

The concept of user authentication goes back in history for millennia, as we humans have found ways to verify our identity. More recent times have seen computer systems adopt these authentication mechanisms and they have now become commonplace on many user devices. These mechanisms often fit into the categories of something we *know*, something we *have*, and something we *are*. Whilst user devices globally run on one or more of these traditional authentication factors, they are not without issue. There are, to name only a few issues, data breaches containing passwords, phishing attacks, biometric spoofing, and lost tokens. The traditional authentication factors also primarily follow the paradigm of authenticating only at the point-of-entry, meaning an attacker stealing or accessing an unlocked user device would have access. Furthermore, some traditional authentication factors require a form of explicit time consuming user interaction, despite studies indicating that authentication is deemed inconvenient because of this. Therefore, to conclude, there are clear issues with traditional authentication mechanisms (e.g., the password) that highlight the need for innovation in the authentication field.

References

1. Akhtar, Z., Micheloni, C., Foresti, G.L.: Biometric liveness detection: challenges and research opportunities. IEEE Security Privacy **13**(5), 63–72 (2015)
2. Al Abdulwahid, A., Clarke, N., Stengel, I., Furnell, S., Reich, C.: Continuous and transparent multimodal authentication: reviewing the state of the art. Cluster Comput. **19**(1), 455–474 (2016)
3. Allan, A.: Passwords are near the breaking point. Gartner Research Note
4. Anderson, R.J.: Security Engineering: A Guide to Building Dependable Distributed Systems, 3 edn. Wiley Publishing, Hoboken (2021)
5. Aviv, A.J., Gibson, K., Mossop, E., Blaze, M., Smith, J.M.: Smudge attacks on smartphone touch screens. In: Proceedings of the 4th USENIX Conference on Offensive Technologies, WOOT'10, pp. 1–7. USENIX Association, Berkeley (2010)
6. Aviv, A.J., Budzitowski, D., Kuber, R.: Is bigger better? Comparing user-generated passwords on 3x3 vs. 4x4 grid sizes for android's pattern unlock. In: Proceedings of the 31st Annual Computer Security Applications Conference, ACSAC 2015, pp. 301–310. Association for Computing Machinery, New York (2015)
7. Aviv, A.J., Davin, J.T., Wolf, F., Kuber, R.: Towards baselines for shoulder surfing on mobile authentication. In: Proceedings of the 33rd Annual Computer Security Applications Conference, ACSAC 2017, pp. 486–498. Association for Computing Machinery, New York (2017)
8. BBC: Security firm RSA offers to replace securID tokens. https://www.bbc.co.uk/news/technology-13681566
9. Bhagavatula, R., Ur, B., Iacovino, K., Kywe, S.M., Cranor, L.F., Savvides, M.: Biometric authentication on iPhone and android: Usability, perceptions, and influences on adoption. In: Proceedings of the Workshop on Usable Security (USEC) (2015)
10. Biddle, R., Chiasson, S., Van Oorschot, P.: Graphical passwords: learning from the first twelve years. ACM Comput. Surv. **44**(4), 1–41 (2012)
11. Bonneau, J., Shutova, E.: Linguistic properties of multi-word passphrases. In: Proceedings of the 16th International Conference on Financial Cryptography and Data Security, FC'12, pp. 1–12. Springer, Berlin (2012)
12. Bonneau, J., Herley, C., Oorschot, P.C.V., Stajano, F.: The quest to replace passwords: A framework for comparative evaluation of web authentication schemes. In: Proceedings of the 2012 IEEE Symposium on Security and Privacy, SP '12, pp. 553–567. IEEE Computer Society, Washington (2012)
13. Bonneau, J., Preibusch, S., Anderson, R.: A birthday present every eleven wallets? The security of customer-chosen banking pins. In: Keromytis, A.D. (ed.) Financial Cryptography and Data Security, pp. 25–40. Springer, Berlin (2012)

14. Bud, A.: Facing the future: the impact of apple faceID. Biomet. Technol. Today **2018**(1), 5–7 (2018)
15. Cao, K., Jain, A.K.: Hacking Mobile Phones Using 2D Printed Fingerprints (2016)
16. Chin, E., Felt, A.P., Sekar, V., Wagner, D.: Measuring user confidence in smartphone security and privacy. In: Proceedings of the Eighth Symposium on Usable Privacy and Security, SOUPS '12. Association for Computing Machinery, New York (2012)
17. Chugh, T., Cao, K., Jain, A.K.: Fingerprint spoof detection using minutiae-based local patches. In: 2017 IEEE International Joint Conference on Biometrics (IJCB), pp. 581–589 (2017)
18. Clarke, N.: Transparent User Authentication: Biometrics, RFID and Behavioural Profiling, 1st edn. Springer Publishing Company, Cham (2011)
19. Clarke, N., Furnell, S.: Authentication of users on mobile telephones - A survey of attitudes and practices. Comput. Secur. **24**(7), 519–527 (2005)
20. Crawford, H., Renaud, K.: Understanding user perceptions of transparent authentication on a mobile device. J. Trust Manag. **1**(7), 1–28 (2014)
21. Dan, U.: Passwords, passwords everywhere - ncsc.gov.uk. https://www.ncsc.gov.uk/blog-post/passwords-passwords-everywhere
22. Das, A., Bonneau, J., Caesar, M., Borisov, N., Wang, X.: The tangled web of password reuse. In: NDSS (2014)
23. Das, S., Dingman, A., Camp, L.J.: Why Johnny doesn't use two factor a two-phase usability study of the FIDO U2F security key. In: Meiklejohn, S., Sako, K. (eds.) Financial Cryptography and Data Security, pp. 160–179. Springer, Berlin (2018)
24. Dasgupta, D., Roy, A., Nag, A.: Advances in User Authentication, 1st edn. Springer Publishing Company, Cham (2017)
25. de Borde, D.: Selecting a two-factor authentication system. Netw. Security **2007**(7), 17–20 (2007)
26. De Luca, A., Hang, A., von Zezschwitz, E., Hussmann, H.: I feel like I'm taking selfies all day! towards understanding biometric authentication on smartphones. In: Proceedings of the 33rd Annual ACM Conference on Human Factors in Computing Systems, CHI '15, p. 1411–1414. Association for Computing Machinery, New York (2015)
27. de Vries, M., Cross, N., Grant, D.: Design Methodology and Relationships with Science. Nato Science Series D. Springer Netherlands, Berlin (1993)
28. Drimer, S., Murdoch, S.J., Anderson, R.: Optimised to fail: Card readers for online banking. In: Dingledine, R., Golle, P. (eds.) Financial Cryptography and Data Security, pp. 184–200. Springer, Berlin (2009)
29. Dutson, J., Allen, D., Eggett, D., Seamons, K.: Don't punish all of us: Measuring user attitudes about two-factor authentication. In: 2019 IEEE European Symposium on Security and Privacy Workshops (EuroS&PW), pp. 119–128 (2019)
30. Eaton, J.: The political significance of the imperial watchword in the early empire. Greece Rome **58**(1), 48–63 (2011)
31. Egelman, S., Jain, S., Portnoff, R.S., Liao, K., Consolvo, S., Wagner, D.: Are you ready to lock? Understanding user motivations for smartphone locking behaviors. In: Proceedings of the 2014 ACM SIGSAC Conference on Computer and Communications Security, Scottsdale, Arizona, USA, pp. 750–761 (2014)
32. Florêncio, D., Herley, C.: Where do security policies come from? In: Proceedings of the Sixth Symposium on Usable Privacy and Security, SOUPS '10. Association for Computing Machinery, New York (2010)
33. Furnell, S., Clarke, N.: Inhabiting the biometric society. ITNOW **60**(3), 42–43 (2018)
34. Galton, F.: Personal identification and description. Nature **38**(973), 173–177 (1888)
35. Ghorbani Lyastani, S., Schilling, M., Neumayr, M., Backes, M., Bugiel, S.: Is FIDO2 the Kingslayer of user authentication? a comparative usability study of FIDO2 passwordless authentication. In: 2020 IEEE Symposium on Security and Privacy (SP), pp. 268–285 (2020)
36. Goodin, D.: Forum cracks the vintage passwords of Ken Thompson and other Unix pioneers (2019). https://arstechnica.com/information-technology/2019/10/forum-cracks-the-vintage-passwords-of-ken-thompson-and-other-unix-pioneers/

37. Goodin, D.: Why passwords have never been weaker–and crackers have never been stronger
    | ars technica. https://arstechnica.com/information-technology/2012/08/passwords-under-
    assault/4/
38. Harbach, M., von Zezschwitz, E., Fichtner, A., De Luca, A., Smith, M.: It's a hard lock life: a
    field study of smartphone (un)locking behavior and risk perception. In: 10th Symposium On
    Usable Privacy and Security (SOUPS 2014), Menlo Park, CA, pp. 213–230 (2014)
39. Harbach, M., De Luca, A., Egelman, S.: The anatomy of smartphone unlocking: A field study
    of android lock screens. In: Proceedings of the 2016 CHI Conference on Human Factors in
    Computing Systems, CHI '16, p. 4806–4817. Association for Computing Machinery, New
    York (2016)
40. Henry, E.: Classification and Uses of Finger Prints. George Routledge and Sons, Milton Park
    (1900)
41. Herschel, W.: The origin of finger-printing. Nature 98(2458), 268–268 (1916)
42. Hoy, M.B.: Alexa, Siri, Cortana, and more: an introduction to voice assistants. Med. Ref.
    Serv. Quart. 37(1), 81–88 (2018)
43. Huseynov, E., Seigneur, J.M.: Context-aware multifactor authentication survey. In: Computer
    and Information Security Handbook, pp. 715–726. Morgan Kaufmann Publishers, Burlington
    (2017)
44. Inglesant, P.G., Sasse, M.A.: The true cost of unusable password policies: Password use in the
    wild. In: Proceedings of the SIGCHI Conference on Human Factors in Computing Systems,
    CHI '10, p. 383–392. Association for Computing Machinery, New York (2010)
45. Jacomme, C., Kremer, S.: An extensive formal analysis of multi-factor authentication
    protocols. ACM Trans. Priv. Secur. 24(2), 1–34 (2021)
46. Jain, A.K., Ross, A., Prabhakar, S.: An introduction to biometric recognition. IEEE Trans.
    Circuits Syst. Video Technol. 14(1), 4–20 (2004)
47. Jain, A.K., Ross, A.A., Nandakumar, K.: Introduction to Biometrics. Springer Publishing
    Company, Cham (2011)
48. Jakobsson, M., Liu, D.: Your Password is Your New PIN, pp. 25–36. Springer, New York
    (2013)
49. Jia, Y., Zhang, Y., Weiss, R.J., Wang, Q., Shen, J., Ren, F., Chen, Z., Nguyen, P., Pang, R.,
    Moreno, I.L., Wu, Y.: Transfer learning from speaker verification to multispeaker text-to-
    speech synthesis. In: Proceedings of the 32nd International Conference on Neural Information
    Processing Systems, NIPS'18, p. 4485–4495. Curran Associates, Red Hook (2018)
50. Jo, H.-H., Karsai, M., Kertesz, J., Kaski, K.: Circadian pattern and burstiness in mobile phone
    communication. New J. Phys. 14(1), 1–17 (2012)
51. Katsini, C., Belk, M., Fidas, C., Avouris, N., Samaras, G.: Security and usability in
    knowledge-based user authentication: A review. In: Proceedings of the 20th Pan Hellenic
    Conference on Informatics, PCI '16. Association for Computing Machinery, New York (2016)
52. Kennedy, W., Olmsted, A.: Three factor authentication. In: 2017 12th International Confer-
    ence for Internet Technology and Secured Transactions (ICITST), pp. 212–213 (2017)
53. Kim, H., Huh, J.H.: Pin selection policies: are they really effective? Comput. Security 31(4),
    484–496 (2012)
54. Koschuch, M., Hudler, M., Eigner, H., Saffer, Z.: Token-based authentication for smart-
    phones. In: 2013 International Conference on Data Communication Networking (DCNET),
    pp. 1–6 (2013)
55. Kuo, C., Romanosky, S., Cranor, L.F.: Human selection of mnemonic phrase-based pass-
    words. In: Proceedings of the Second Symposium on Usable Privacy and Security, SOUPS
    '06, pp. 67–78. Association for Computing Machinery, New York (2006)
56. Li, S.Z., Jain, A.K.: Handbook of Face Recognition, 2nd edn. Springer Publishing Company,
    Cham (2011)
57. Maguire, M.: The birth of biometric security. Anthropol. Today 25(2), 9–14 (2009)
58. Mahfouz, A., Muslukhov, I., Beznosov, K.: Android users in the wild: their authentication
    and usage behavior. Pervasive Mob. Comput. 32, 50–61 (2016)

59. Malone, D., Maher, K.: Investigating the distribution of password choices. In: Proceedings of the 21st International Conference on World Wide Web, WWW '12, p. 301–310. Association for Computing Machinery, New York (2012)
60. Maltoni, D., Maio, D., Jain, A.K., Prabhakar, S.: Handbook of Fingerprint Recognition, 2nd edn. Springer Publishing Company, Cham (2009)
61. Marasco, E., Ross, A.: A survey on antispoofing schemes for fingerprint recognition systems. ACM Comput. Surv. **47**(2), 1–36 (2014)
62. Markert, P., Bailey, D.V., Golla, M., Dürmuth, M., Aviv, A.J.: This pin can be easily guessed: Analyzing the security of smartphone unlock pins. In: 2020 IEEE Symposium on Security and Privacy (SP), pp. 286–303 (2020)
63. Miller, J.B., Trivi, J.M.: Direct, gesture-based actions from device's lock screen (2012)
64. NCSC: The logic behind three random words - ncsc.gov.uk. https://www.ncsc.gov.uk/blog-post/the-logic-behind-three-random-words
65. O'Gorman, L.: Comparing passwords, tokens, and biometrics for user authentication. Proc. IEEE **91**(12), 2021–2040 (2003)
66. Otsuka, Y.: Face recognition in infants: a review of behavioral and near-infrared spectroscopic studies. Japanese Psycholog. Res. **56**(1), 76–90 (2014)
67. Patel, K., Han, H., Jain, A.K.: Secure face unlock: spoof detection on smartphones. IEEE Trans. Informat. Forens. Security **11**(10), 2268–2283 (2016)
68. Pearman, S., Thomas, J., Naeini, P.E., Habib, H., Bauer, L., Christin, N., Cranor, L.F., Egelman, S., Forget, A.: Let's go in for a closer look: Observing passwords in their natural habitat. In: Proceedings of the 2017 ACM SIGSAC Conference on Computer and Communications Security, CCS '17, p. 295–310. Association for Computing Machinery, New York (2017)
69. Porter, S.N.: A password extension for improved human factors. Comput. Security **1**(1), 54–56 (1982)
70. Puce, A.: Face recognition: Psychological and neural aspects. In: Smelser, N.J., Baltes, P.B. (eds.) International Encyclopedia of the Social & Behavioral Sciences, pp. 5226–5230. Pergamon, Oxford (2001)
71. Rabkin, A.: Personal knowledge questions for fallback authentication: Security questions in the era of Facebook. In: Proceedings of the 4th Symposium on Usable Privacy and Security, SOUPS '08, p. 13–23. Association for Computing Machinery, New York (2008)
72. Rasnayaka, S., Saha, S., Sim, T.: Making the most of what you have! Profiling biometric authentication on mobile devices. In: International Conference on Biometrics (ICB) 2019, Crete, Greece, pp. 1–7 (2019)
73. Renaud, K., Otondo, R., Warkentin, M.: "this is the way 'i' create my passwords" ...does the endowment effect deter people from changing the way they create their passwords? Comput. Security **82**, 241–260 (2019)
74. Salahdine, F., Kaabouch, N.: Social engineering attacks: a survey. Future Int. **11**(4), 89 (2019)
75. Samangouei, P., Patel, V.M., Chellappa, R.: Facial attributes for active authentication on mobile devices. Image Vision Comput. **58**, 181–192 (2017)
76. Sasse, M.A., Brostoff, S., Weirich, D.: Transforming the 'weakest link' — a human/computer interaction approach to usable and effective security. BT Technol. J. **19**(3), 122–131 (2001)
77. Schneier, B.: Inside risks: semantic network attacks. Commun. ACM **43**(12), 168 (2000)
78. Schneier, B.: Secrets & Lies: Digital Security in a Networked World, 1st edn. Wiley, Hoboken (2000)
79. Schneier, B.: We Have Root: Even More Advice from Schneier on Security. Wiley, Hoboken (2019)
80. Sethi, I.K.: Biometrics, pp. 117–134. Springer US, Boston (2006)
81. Shah, S.W., Kanhere, S.S.: Recent trends in user authentication—a survey. IEEE Access **7**, 112505–112519 (2019)
82. Shakespeare, W., Raffel, B., Bloom, H.: Hamlet. Yale University Press, New Have (2003)

83. Simon, L., Anderson, R.: Pin skimmer: Inferring pins through the camera and microphone. In: Proceedings of the Third ACM Workshop on Security and Privacy in Smartphones & Mobile Devices, SPSM '13, pp. 67–78. Association for Computing Machinery, New York (2013)

84. Singha, R.: The great war and a 'proper' passport for the colony: Border-crossing in British India, c.1882–1922. Indian Econ. Soc. History Rev. **50**(3), 289–315 (2013)

85. Standing, L., Conezio, J., Haber, R.N.: Perception and memory for pictures: single-trial learning of 2500 visual stimuli. Psychon. Sci. **19**(2), 73–74 (1970)

86. Stobert, E., Biddle, R.: The password life cycle. ACM Trans. Priv. Secur. **21**(3), 1–32 (2018)

87. Sun, C., Wang, Y., Zheng, J.: Dissecting pattern unlock: the effect of pattern strength meter on pattern selection. J. Informat. Security Appl. **19**(4), 308–320 (2014)

88. Teh, P.S., Zhang, N., Tan, S.Y., Shi, Q., Khoh, W.H., Nawaz, R.: Strengthen user authentication on mobile devices by using user's touch dynamics pattern. J. Ambient Intell. Humaniz. Comput. **11**(10), 4019–4039 (2020)

89. Uellenbeck, S., Dürmuth, M., Wolf, C., Holz, T.: Quantifying the security of graphical passwords: The case of android unlock patterns. In: Proceedings of the 2013 ACM SIGSAC Conference on Computer & Communications Security, CCS '13, p. 161–172. Association for Computing Machinery, New York (2013)

90. Ulqinaku, E., Assal, H., Abdou, A., Chiasson, S., Čapkun, S.: Is real-time phishing eliminated with FIDO? Social engineering downgrade attacks against fido protocols. Cryptology ePrint Archive, Report 2020/1298 (2020). https://eprint.iacr.org/2020/1298

91. Ur, B., Noma, F., Bees, J., Segreti, S.M., Shay, R., Bauer, L., Christin, N., Cranor, L.F.: "i added '!' at the end to make it secure": Observing password creation in the lab. In: Proceedings of the Eleventh USENIX Conference on Usable Privacy and Security, SOUPS '15, pp. 123–140. USENIX Association, Berkeley (2015)

92. Ur, B., Segreti, S.M., Bauer, L., Christin, N., Cranor, L.F., Komanduri, S., Kurilova, D., Mazurek, M.L., Melicher, W., Shay, R.: Measuring real-world accuracies and biases in modeling password guessability. In: Proceedings of the 24th USENIX Conference on Security Symposium, SEC'15, pp. 463–481. USENIX Association, Berkeley (2015)

93. van Oorschot, P.C.: Computer Security and the Internet. Springer, Berlin (2020)

94. Vittori, P.: Ultimate password: is voice the best biometric to beat hackers? Biometr. Technol. Today **2019**(9), 8–10 (2019)

95. von Zezschwitz, E., Dunphy, P., De Luca, A.: Patterns in the wild: a field study of the usability of pattern and PIN-based authentication on mobile devices. In: Proceedings of Mobile HCI 2013 - Security And Privacy, pp. 261–270. Munich, Germany (2013)

96. von Zezschwitz, E., Eiband, M., Buschek, D., Oberhuber, S., De Luca, A., Alt, F., Hussmann, H.: On quantifying the effective password space of grid-based unlock gestures. In: Proceedings of the 15th International Conference on Mobile and Ubiquitous Multimedia, MUM '16, p. 201–212. Association for Computing Machinery, New York (2016)

97. Wang, D., Cheng, H., Wang, P., Huang, X., Jian, G.: Zipf's law in passwords. IEEE Trans. Informat. Forens. Security **12**(11), 2776–2791 (2017)

98. Wayman, J.L., Jain, A.K., Maltoni, D., Maio, D.: Biometric Systems: Technology, Design and Performance Evaluation. Springer Science & Business Media, Cham (2005)

99. Wen, D., Han, H., Jain, A.K.: Face spoof detection with image distortion analysis. IEEE Trans. Informat. Forens. Security **10**(4), 746–761 (2015)

100. Woodward, J.D., Orlans, N.M., Higgins, P.T.: Biometrics: Identity Assurance in the Information Age. McGraw-Hill/Osborne, New York, NY (2003)

101. Yang, Y., Yeo, K.C., Azam, S., Karim, A., Ahammad, R., Mahmud, R.: Empirical study of password strength meter design. In: 2020 5th International Conference on Communication and Electronics Systems (ICCES), pp. 436–442 (2020)

102. Ye, G., Tang, Z., Fang, D., Chen, X., Kim, K., Taylor, B., Wang, Z.: Cracking android pattern lock in five attempts. In: Proceedings 2017 Network and Distributed System Security Symposium 2017 (NDSS'17), pp. 0–0. Internet Society, Reston (2017)

103. Zhang, G., Yan, C., Ji, X., Zhang, T., Zhang, T., Xu, W.: Dolphinattack: Inaudible voice commands. In: Proceedings of the 2017 ACM SIGSAC Conference on Computer and Communications Security, CCS '17, p. 103–117. Association for Computing Machinery, New York (2017)

104. Zhou, B., Xie, Z., Zhang, Y., Lohokare, J., Gao, R., Ye, F.: Robust human face authentication leveraging acoustic sensing on smartphones. IEEE Trans. Mob. Comput. **21**, 1–1 (2021)

105. Zhuang, L., Zhou, F., Tygar, J.D.: Keyboard acoustic emanations revisited. ACM Trans. Inf. Syst. Secur. **13**(1), 1–26 (2009)

106. Zirjawi, N., Kurtanovic, Z., Maalej, W.: A survey about user requirements for biometric authentication on smartphones. In 2015 IEEE 2nd Workshop on Evolving Security and Privacy Requirements Engineering (ESPRE), Ottawa, Canada, pp. 1–6 (2015)

Chapter 3
Continuous Authentication

3.1 Introduction

User authentication on user devices began with knowledge-based authentication techniques (such as passwords), which continue to be utilised on most devices. However, these techniques have known weaknesses; users often select simplistic forms of secret knowledge that can render them susceptible to types of capture and guessing attacks and enable attackers to learn the secret knowledge (see Sect. 2.3.1). One of the few recent advancements in user authentication is the use of biometrics (such as fingerprints) obtained via dedicated sensors to authenticate users. The use of biometrics alleviates the issues with weak secret knowledge but comes with other issues such as spoof attacks (see Sect. 2.3.1).

The implementation comes with a further corollary in that authenticating once assumes that all unprotected data on the device (pictures, messages, applications, etc.) requires an equal level of security [28]. In practice some resources (such as emails) may have higher security requirements than others (such as games). The current authentication techniques do not contain the nuance to apply different levels of authentication to different resources and adopt a one-size-fits-all paradigm [48]. Given the security requirements for a resource, this may result in the authentication being too weak (risking security and the possibility of impostor access) or too strong (risking usability through the intrusiveness of authentication).

Furthermore, modern devices generally rely on a single form of authentication, such as single piece of secret knowledge (e.g., a PIN) or a single biometric (e.g., a fingerprint). Whilst multi-factor authentication carries security benefits it can intrude on usability (by increasing the authentication burden on the user) and is generally omitted from default authentication options. However, relying only on a single form of authentication becomes a single point of failure because an attacker would only need to bypass one authentication mechanism. There is also an issue for usability in relying on a single form of authentication; if a user forgets their secret

© The Author(s), under exclusive license to Springer Nature Switzerland AG 2024
M. Smith-Creasey, *Continuous Biometric Authentication Systems*, SpringerBriefs in Computer Science, https://doi.org/10.1007/978-3-031-49071-2_3

knowledge or a biometric sensor collects data from previously unseen contexts (e.g., faces in poorly illuminated areas) then authentication can be hindered.

There also exists the issue of fallback attacks in modern device authentication systems employing biometrics. In the event that the biometrics are not authenticated, some systems fallback to knowledge-based authentication such as a PIN. Given that biometric systems such as FaceID claim a false acceptance rate of 1 in 1,000,000 [27] and a 4-digit PIN has a false acceptance rate of 1 in 10,000 that can be attacked via knowledge known about the user, it may be the case that the PIN is easier for an attacker to crack. It can also effectively be bypassed in a fallback attack by reverting to a form of knowledge-based authentication (likely easier for an attacker to crack).

The advancements in hardware over the past few decades have seen device speed, portability, and capabilities increase, which has facilitated changes in user interaction. The interconnectivity of applications and services (e.g., social media) has provided frequent and real-time notifications on user devices. This has led to device usage being built around smaller and more frequent sessions. This behaviour is especially prominent on smartphones where users can have many sessions throughout the day, sometimes lasting only seconds. The current authentication mechanisms can be inconvenient when used to authenticate this form of interaction; knowledge-based authentication (e.g., a password) can take up to 4.7 seconds to input on a smartphone and a biometric (e.g., a face) may require the device picked up and held in front of the face. Some smartphone users find traditional authentication awkward [18] or inconvenient resulting in some disabling authentication altogether.

The portability of devices also presents new threats to the devices and the data stored (or accessible) on them via loss or theft. Recent reports suggest thieves are targeting in-use devices (due to a higher black market value if stolen whilst unlocked) [35]. The Crime Survey for England & Wales revealed an estimated 325,000 smartphone thefts in the year up to March 2020 [54] and prominent UK government departments had 2004 devices lost or stolen in a 12-month period ending June 2019 [8]. However, although portability sees such devices face greater risk of theft or loss than older static terminal computers of earlier times, many rely on the same authentication paradigms. This authentication paradigm sees authentication at the point-of-entry as the only authentication mechanism.

Users are aware of some of the security risks to leaving devices vulnerable and unlocked but have been shown to do so anyway [9]. Whilst it is easy to assume users are ambivalent about device security due to their poor authentication choices and decisions, it must be acknowledged that users *do* desire security to keep their data safe. It is often one of the top user requirements for devices and services today when users are surveyed. It is simply the case that users also place high importance on convenience. However, the requirements for security and usability often conflict and some users will sacrifice security for usability (e.g., reusing PINs or passwords across different devices or services).

Recent research efforts have produced *continuous authentication* systems that can solve many issues of traditional forms of authentication. These systems require frequent evidence from the user that matches the claimed identity to continuously authenticate. Many biometrics, such as the face, may be collected both continuously and transparently which makes them an ideal authentication factor for continuous authentication systems [14]. These systems improve on traditional authentication techniques by providing both enhanced security (e.g., authenticating beyond the point-of-entry) *and* enhanced usability (e.g., via non-intrusive biometric collection).

These continuous authentication systems function by continuously capturing one or more biometrics. Over an enrolment period (which may vary from seconds to days depending on the biometric) the biometrics are used to build a user profile. In subsequent usage the continuously collected biometrics are compared to the user profile to produce a score that is evaluated against a threshold. This comparison is often done at a high frequency, possibly for every biometric reading or a window of readings collected over a time period. If the comparison finds a score is below the threshold, then remedial action can be taken in real-time. This remedial action may be to degrade a device trust score, restrict access to certain resources, or lock the device entirely. This process continues throughout the usage of the device.

Continuous authentication has advantages not present in traditional authentication schemes that increases the security of such systems. The use of biometrics removes the risk of the authenticator being observed or stolen, as is possible in knowledge-based and possession-based authentication solutions. Many recent continuous biometric authentication schemes also make use of multiple biometrics which can enable enhanced accuracies and increase the burden on attackers that may wish to spoof the system [77]. Unlike traditional forms of authentication which rely primarily on physiological biometrics (such as faces and fingerprints), continuous authentication can also utilise behavioural biometrics which can be more difficult to spoof. These systems have also shown to be rated highly in terms of both security and usability by users (unlike some traditional forms of authentication).

Despite the recent prominence of the field, continuous authentication is not a new concept and has been written about as early as 1995 where a solution was based on user typing behaviour [71]. However, since then devices have become more computationally powerful, machine learning techniques have progressed, and sensors from which high-quality biometrics can be obtained have become commonplace on devices. This has led to an increase of continuous authentication systems proposed in the last decade that have potential to become viable mainstream forms of authentication. The following sections explore how continuous authentication systems are constructed, and the similarities and differences in how they function.

3.2 Concept

The concept of continuous biometric authentication is broad because of the diversity of the solutions that have been proposed to authenticate users. The term *continuous authentication* is now prominent to describe such systems, but such techniques have also been referred to as *transparent, implicit, active, non-intrusive, unobtrusive,* and *non-observable* authentication [1]. Throughout the evolution of continuous authentication, multiple definitions have been provided by different studies and researchers.

The definitions provided in the related literature include the following:

- A system where 'biometric verification is not merely used to authenticate a session on startup, but that it is used in a loop throughout the session to continuously authenticate the presence/participation of the user' [72].
- System 'continuously checks the identity of the user throughout the session' [4].
- System to 'monitor the user's interaction with the device, and ideally, at every point in time (or at least with a high frequency) the system estimates if the legitimate user is using the device. Hence, a continuous authentication method can either complement entry-point based authentication methods by monitoring the user after a successful login or, if the method satisfies particular accuracy requirements, it could even substitute entry-point based authentication' [26].
- A security mechanism that can 'continuously monitor user behaviour and use this as basis to re-authenticate them periodically throughout a login session' [80].
- System that 'attempts to authenticate the user periodically after the log-in' [68].
- A system 'that monitors user actions at every point in time (or at least with a high frequency) during a session and determines if that user is the legitimate one. If it is not the case, suitable defensive mechanisms should be put in place' [31].

Whilst the above definitions are different, they can be used to derive the key commonalities of a continuous biometric authentication system. Firstly, it is required for the system to authenticate the user frequently/periodically throughout a usage session in a continuous loop. Secondly, it must utilise one or more biometric traits to decide if the user is legitimate. Thirdly, action should be taken if the user is deemed illegitimate. The above definitions and the commonalities between them are used here to define continuous biometric authentication for user devices as a security mechanism that collects one or more behavioural and/or physiological biometrics continuously (or at least with high frequency) beyond a potential initial point-of-entry and throughout a session, such that they can be matched against a genuine user profile to determine and implement an access policy.

3.2.1 Components

A continuous biometric authentication system can be implemented in a wide variety of ways. There are a range of different variables to consider when creating such a system. These include the biometric modalities, classification techniques, and policy decisions that might be implemented depending on the security requirements. Some of these systems will be of greater complexity than others and require more sophisticated components to operate optimally. However, there are some common components that most systems will require as a bare minimum to function. Various works have discussed the components common to a continuous biometric authentication system, with similar components listed in [4], [14], and [45]. There is an overlap of these components with those found in standard (i.e., one-shot) biometric authentication approaches [39]. The following describes the components.

- **Capture**: The capture component (also called the acquisition module [45] or sensor module [4]) is the component that captures raw sensor data. This raw data will vary depending on the type of sensor (e.g., a touchscreen will provide x and y coordinates, whereas an accelerometer will provide tri-axis x, y, and z readings). The raw sensor data can be difficult to use directly in classification processes and will usually go through pre-processing or feature extraction first.
- **Extraction**: The extraction component (also more explicitly called the feature extraction module [45]) is dedicated to extracting a compact but expressive digital representation of the underlying biometric trait [39]. The subsequent features are often stored within a *feature vector*. There will often need to be a pre-processing stage prior to extraction that may include quality assessment, segmentation, and enhancement [39]. This process is done for both enrolment and authentication.
- **Storage**: The storage component (also called the database module [39], biometric database [4], or feature templates [45]) is an element that stores the enrolled biometric information. This storage may contain the biometric feature vectors or a trained machine learning model representative of the biometric information. The storage component is used when a genuine user's biometric is needed for comparison. This storage is often local and on the user's device.
- **Classification**: The classification component (also called the matching module [39]) is the component responsible for generating a similarity score between some captured biometric sample and the enrolled biometric data. The classification component will often be implemented via a distance measure (e.g., Euclidean distance) or machine learning techniques (e.g., random forest classifiers). Different classification approaches will often suit different biometric traits.
- **Decision**: The decision component (also called the response unit [4]) is the component that forms the final decision as to what action should be taken based on the biometric samples captured. The decision component will usually utilise a threshold that scores from the classification component are compared to. The decision component will enforce policies based on if the score is above or below the threshold. Scores below the threshold usually result in restricted access.

3.2.2 Architecture

The concept of a continuous biometric authentication system requires an architecture based upon the aforementioned components. This architecture must also incorporate the key characteristics of such a system (described in Sect. 3.2) such that it forms a continuous loop, utilises one or more biometric traits, and takes a decision based on a match score. Despite these requirements, there are a variety of ways in which such an architecture might be implemented (e.g., a storage component might device-based or cloud-based). Therefore, this discussion is focused on a high-level approach to the architecture in which technical and implementation options are omitted.

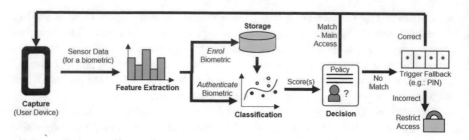

Fig. 3.1 The architecture and components of a typical continuous biometric authentication system

Firstly, the architecture must reflect the necessity of the system to collect biometric information from some sensing capabilities on a user device for the purpose of initial enrolment and subsequent authentication. Secondly, the architecture must reflect a stage at which the captured sensing information goes through any preprocessing and feature extraction stages before it is used. The architecture must then reflect the storage of these features (or any machine learning model subsequently trained on these features). It must then be reflected that a classification process must occur in which the feature vectors collected and computed for authentication are compared to those enrolled in the system provide a similarity score. Then, the architecture must reflect that the system must make an access decision based on the score and any associated security policies. Finally, the architecture must reflect that (at least during access) the authentication process must continue indefinitely. Figure 3.1 shows a high-level and system-agnostic architecture satisfying these requirements.

3.3 User Devices

Advances in device technology have enabled the development of continuous biometric authentication systems. The processing power of computing devices has progressed exponentially in recent decades. This has generally followed *Moore's law*, the observation that transistors on integrated circuits appeared to double every 2 years (a law which may not apply so accurately in future [69]). Today, at our fingertips in our smartphones and tablets, we hold many times the amount of processing power than was available for Apollo 11 to take mankind to the Moon on July 16, 1969 [86]. As this processing power has increased, however, the cost of processing power has also decreased [63]. This trend has enabled a shift from large industrial computers used for specialist purposes (e.g., business or military) to smaller and affordable consumer devices like the ones at desks, in pockets, and on wrists.

The last few decades have seen the rise of many personal use computing devices, distinct from those marketed to businesses. These devices have also become smaller, and therefore more portable, but contain greater functionality. The connectivity and access to information, enabled by the Internet and the World Wide Web (pioneered by Tim Berners-Lee at CERN in 1989), provided devices with the ability to browse almost anything. This has been further facilitated by mobile wireless telecommunications technologies, such as 4G and 5G, that have provided many users connectivity almost anywhere. These factors have made a plethora of different devices a staple in everyday life, for both personal and professional use.

3.3.1   Device Types

Continuous biometric authentication systems were first proposed for desktop computer systems (specifically, the IBM PC [71]). Such systems have since been developed for a variety of devices. The primary device focus here is *user devices*. These user devices are treated as those computing devices with which a user will regularly interact with to fulfil a certain task. Many of these user devices generally require a form of authentication and provide access to some form of information. The user devices optimal for continuous biometric authentication will generally be used regularly, have high-frequency sensing capabilities, contain adequate processing power, and have an appropriate power source or battery. This, therefore, excludes some Internet-of-Things devices. In [64], the authors divide devices used for continuous authentication into four categories: (i) mobile devices (including smartphones and tablets), (ii) personal computers (such as desktop and laptops), (iii) wearables (and other devices in the Internet-of-Things), and (iv) other devices. The following describes this non-exhaustive list of devices types suitable for continuous authentication.

- **Personal Computers**: Personal computers are devices such as laptop and desktop computers [64]. These devices are generally some of the most computationally powerful user devices (in terms of CPU and GPU), enabled by their larger size when compared to mobile or wearable devices. Users will generally interact with these devices via a keyboard and a mouse and sometimes also via a webcam and a microphone. These devices have seen huge adoption over the past decades. In 1985 the percentage of households with home computers was only 13%. By 2000 this had increased to 44%, and by 2015 it had increased to 88%. The significant processing power, multiple sensing capabilities, and large market penetration makes personal computers an optimal device for continuous authentication.
- **Mobile Devices**: Mobile devices are generally types of devices that are extremely portable, have Internet connectivity, and can be operated via a touchscreen. Both smartphone and tablet devices are grouped within this category [64]. Smartphones, in particular, have seen rapid adoption since the late 2000s. In a 2019 consumer survey it was reported that in 2012 smartphone usage in the UK was 52%, but by 2019 this had reached 88% and had hit a natural plateau,

increasing by only 1% since the prior year. Such an adoption level is higher than that of both laptops and tablets. The survey finds that the market is still incredibly active with 1.4 billion devices shipped in 2019 and likely investment in new processors, machine learning capabilities, computational photography, display technology, and connectivity. Mobile devices are usually equipped with a significant array of sensing capabilities (often more so than desktop or laptop computers). These capabilities provide access to a variety of data suitable for continuous authentication systems.

- **Wearables**: Wearable devices are, simply, computing devices that are worn upon one's person in order to fulfil one or more tasks. Wearables have seen significant development in the 2010s, with wrist-worn devices from companies such as *Fitbit* and *Apple* coming to the market. Such devices are generally setup and managed via another device (e.g., a smartphone) which they connect to via Bluetooth. Many of these devices are marketed as providing fitness features, often utilising sensors to detect movement. More advanced devices can also provide other functionalities (e.g., allowing for messaging and telephone calls). Since *Fitbit* released their first wrist-worn activity tracker in 2013, the market has been growing. There were 28.8 million wearable shipments worldwide in 2014. However, by 2021 this had reached 533.6 million. Whilst there is often limited data on many wearables when compared with a smartphone or laptop, continuous authentication could still be used to utilise the device sensors to protect against unauthorised access.

- **Other**: There are an abundance of other devices that require authentication and have a variety of sensing capabilities. One such device gaining popularity is the virtual reality (VR) headset. These devices (coupled with the controllers) allow the collection of movement data that may be used to continuously authenticate users during usage [74]. Many other devices might be considered for a continuous authentication system if they have adequate processing power, access to machine learning, an ample battery or power source, and rich sensing capabilities.

3.3.2 Sensing Capabilities

Any device for which a continuous authentication system is being designed requires sensing capabilities. Without sensing capabilities (whether that is data from hardware-based sensors or software-based monitoring) a continuous authentication scheme would not be able to derive the biometrics it requires to operate. There are a variety of sensing capabilities offered on devices today. These differ based on the type of device and the purpose of the device. For example, stationary devices may be unlikely to have sensors to monitor movement (e.g., accelerometers).

In recent times there has been an increase of sensors on modern devices. For example, in the space of a decade mobile phones have gone from devices with limited sensing capacity to devices that include touchscreens, GPS, cameras, and more. The use of these sensors does, of course, make the assumption that they are correctly calibrated and trusted (e.g., they have not been compromised by injection attacks [32]). The following lists sensors seen on some user devices.

- **Accelerometer**: The accelerometer measures the acceleration force on a device (in m/s^2) on all three x, y, and z axes (often excluding gravity). This information can be used to detect different activities (such as walking). These sensors are common in smartphones, tablet computers, and fitness wearables.
- **Gyroscope**: The gyroscope sensor measures the rate of rotation of the device (in rad/s) around each physical x, y, and z axis. This can be useful in detecting subtle rotation patterns in device use (e.g., when the device is switched from portrait to landscape). These sensors are often found in tablets and smartphones.
- **Magnetometer**: The magnetometer measures the ambient magnetic field around the device (in μT) for all three the physical axes x, y, and z. The magnetometer can be used as a compass, making use of the magnetic field of the Earth (generated by the motion of molten iron in the core). These are common in smartphones.
- **Touchscreen**: The touchscreens on most devices are capacitive, consisting of a glass panel coated with a transparent conductor that responds to touch from the human body as an electrical conductor. The concept was pioneered at CERN in the 1970s by Frank Beck and Bent Stumpe. These sensors provide x and y coordinates. They are found in smartphones, tablets, wearables, and laptops.
- **Microphone**: The microphone is a sensor that converts sounds within the local environment to electrical signals. Most smaller microphones on modern user devices are MEMS (microelectromechanical system) microphones. The microphone is often used for voice calls on almost all modern user devices.
- **Camera**: The camera is an optical sensor that enables the capture of images. On modern devices a lens focuses light onto a sensor of pixels allowing for the light to be converted into a digital image. Over the last decade, cameras on user devices (e.g., smartphones, laptops, and tablets) have seen considerable development and are capable of capturing high-quality images and video.
- **Ambient Light**: The ambient light sensor measures the ambient light in the surrounding environment of a device in lux (lx). This sensor is common on many modern user devices and is generally used to adjust the brightness of the screen according to the ambient light so as to optimise brightness and battery life.
- **Mouse Movement**: The mouse (or trackpad on laptops) is an input sensor that utilises motion to manipulate an on-screen pointer around a two-dimensional workspace. This is generally found on personal computers and laptop devices.
- **Keyboard**: The computer keyboard is an input sensor that enables the input of characters into a system. These have been implemented via hardware for personal computers and laptops but have more recently been implemented via software on user devices with touchscreens such as smartphones and tablets.
- **Bluetooth**: The Bluetooth sensor on a device uses radio waves for short-range wireless communication between devices. This capability is included on many user devices (e.g., laptops, tablets, smartphones, and smartwatches) to allow simple connection between devices and building personal area networks (PANs).

- **Wi-fi**: The Wi-fi protocol allows devices to use radio waves to connect to a local network, often then allowing the devices access to the Internet. The Wi-fi capability is found on almost all modern wireless devices (e.g., smartphones, laptops, etc.) and allows users to select local networks broadcasting their identifier.
- **Global Positioning System (GPS)**: The GPS sensors on devices obtain signals from satellites containing information from which the location of the device can be derived. This technology has been seen on a plethora of portable user devices including smartphones, smartwatches, and tablets.
- **Heart Rate**: Heart rate sensing often utilises photoplethysmography. This is a method of measuring the heart rate through the fluctuations in blood volume as recognised via reflections from a green light emitted at a high frequency. The blood volume, and therefore heart rate, is deduced by the intensity of the reflections. This is commonly seen in smartwatches and fitness trackers.
- **Cellular**: The cellular capability allows devices to connect to local cell towers. The device communicates signals to the cell tower via radio waves and the cell tower subsequently uses the cellular network to transfer these signals to a recipient. This capability allows user devices such as smartphones, smartwatches, and tablets to send calls, text messages, and data.
- **Barometer**: The barometer is a sensor that measures the ambient air pressure, often in hectopascals (hPa) or millibars ($mbar$). The average pressure at sea level is 1013.25 mbar. The readings might be used to detect changes in weather or altitude. These sensors are often found in smartphones and smartwatches.
- **Fingerprint Scanner**: The fingerprint scanner can be implemented in a variety of ways (e.g., via capacitive sensors). They obtain a digital representation of a fingerprint when the finger is presented to the sensor. These sensors are found on many user devices (e.g., smartphones, smartwatches, laptops, and tablets) and are used to authenticate users attempting to gain access.
- **Proximity**: The proximity sensor detects the proximity of the device to another object. This is often implemented as an infrared LED and an infrared sensor. The greater the intensity of infrared light reflected to the sensor, the closer the proximity estimation. These sensors are commonly found on smartphones to turn off the screen when against the user's ear or in the user's pocket.
- **System/Application Statistics**: The system and application statistics are a capability that records (or allows for the recording of) general device usage. These might include access times, CPU usage, Internet traffic, and device settings. These statistics are usually captured via software and available on most user devices.

The above sensing capabilities can provide information about factors relating to the user, the device, or the environment. Some of these sensing capabilities can provide biometrics that can be useful in a continuous authentication system. However, it is worth noting that not all sensing capabilities are equal and some will provide more accurate, quality, and distinct biometric information than others. Furthermore, these sensing capabilities come at different costs to the power consumption of the device. In [58], the authors found that the camera consumed the most power, followed by the microphone, then the accelerometer, and, lastly, the touchscreen. To reduce the power consumption of some sensing capabilities, the sampling rate can sometimes be adjusted with minimal detriment to the error rate [49]. Furthermore, resource profile curves (RPCs) might be used to evaluate the trade-off between authentication accuracy and power usage, allowing for the system to intelligently adapt between different biometrics depending on the security requirements [58].

3.4 Datasets

The creation of a functional continuous biometric authentication system requires data from sensors during regular device use such that the system can enrol and authenticate the user. In practice, this collection would be initiated as the user activates the continuous authentication system on their device. Some biometric traits will require longer to collect enough training data for than others (e.g., facial biometrics may only require several images, whereas touchscreen-based authentication may require hours of screen interactions). It should also be the case that only the genuine user uses the device during the enrolment phase, otherwise the profile may contain the biometric data of others and authenticate poorly. Many current continuous biometric authentication systems are constructed for research purposes and are, therefore, based on pre-collected datasets for experimentation. There are some important data acquisition considerations to note and some public datasets that might be useful.

3.4.1 Data Acquisition

In order to perform experiments emulating a continuous authentication scheme, it is necessary to acquire data of device usage. The collection process of data which is used in continuous biometric authentication studies can be of variable quality for numerous reasons. The number of participants that are used in each study differs immensely. Some studies will provide limited proof-of-concept results on a minimal set of users, whereas other studies will include a greater number of users to provide results with greater robustness and reliability. It is also the case that studies containing data collected over a greater breadth of time and context can benefit the creation of a more well-rounded user profile with greater nuance. These aspects must be considered when producing a real-world system, though producing high-quality datasets can require time (e.g., for collection) and expense (e.g., for equipment).

Many studies will class their data as being collected from either *controlled* or *uncontrolled* environments. The concept of controlled environments refers to those in which the user is, to an extent, constrained as to what they can do. Such environments often require a user to perform a certain task, such as in [26] where users had to play a 'spot the difference' game. Conversely, the concept of uncontrolled environments are those that have no constraints on what the user can do with the device, such as in [40] where users were allowed to interact with the device as they ordinarily would. The benefit of an uncontrolled environment is that it can better reflect real-world usage, capturing nuances that might not be present in controlled environments.

When collecting data in a controlled environment there might be multiple collection sessions. The number of sessions determines whether the dataset collected is considered inter-session or intra-session. Data that is intra-session collects data from a single session, and data that is inter-session collects data from two or more sessions. Datasets containing intra-session data might be collected faster than those containing inter-session data but do suffer from the potential of bias introduced during that single session that might not be present in future. Inter-session datasets contain multiple sessions which have the advantage of reducing potential session-based bias. In [26] the authors showed a reduction in accuracy in inter-session data in which the test data was collected a week after the training data.

The technical level of data acquisition often requires a computer application to collect and store data. This could be an application written for the Android operating system utilising Java/Kotlin and requesting the use of the Android functionality via permissions.[1] Similarly, this could be a Python or Java program for a Windows/macOS computer that collects data during use. When creating a program for data collection, it is important to consult the supervisors or principal investigators of the study to ensure any appropriate procedure is followed. Furthermore, there could be some regulations relevant to the area that may be consulted (see Sect. 5.7).

3.4.2 Datasets

Some researchers that have collected a dataset for their research have subsequently released them (often with conditions) into the public domain for other researchers to conduct similar experiments. This approach to research can be beneficial because it can improve the likelihood of fair comparison between experiments utilising the same datasets. For example, a dataset used and publicly released by a popular touchscreen-based gesture study in 2013 [26] has subsequently been utilised in numerous other studies in attempts to improve on the results with different techniques.

Several popular and available datasets are displayed and described in Table 3.1. When using a dataset that is available publicly, it is important to note any conditions that come with using the dataset (e.g., some datasets will have restrictions on

---

[1] https://developer.android.com/guide/topics/permissions/overview.

Table 3.1 Some of the shared datasets available (sometimes subject to certain conditions) to researchers that could be used to conduct continuous biometric authentication research. Notice the variation in sensor data, number of users, and duration of data collection in the datasets

Dataset	Year	Device type	Sensors(s)	Users	Duration
Touchalytics [26]	2013	Smartphone	Touchscreen	41	<50 mins
H-MOG [73]	2016	Smartphone	Touchscreen, accel., gyro., magnet.	100	Several days
GCU [40]	2013	Smartphone	App use, Wi-Fi, cell, CPU, light, noise, magnet., gyro.	7	<3 weeks
Rice [70]	2010	Smartphone	App use, Wi-Fi, cell, device activity, call history, battery, CPU, accelerometer	25	12 months
MIT [20]	2004	Smartphone	App use, Bluetooth, cell towers, device activity, calls, device charge	100	6 months
Keyboard Dynamics [42]	2009	PC	Keyboard interactions	51	8+ days
Clarkson II [52]	2017	PC	Keyboard interactions, mouse movements, software programs	103	2.5 years
Clarkson [83]	2014	PC	Keyboard interactions, video of facial expressions, video of hand movements	39	2 days
WISDM [85]	2019	Smartphone & Smartwatch	Accelerometer & gyroscope	51	<1 hour

commercial use). It is also important to note the limitations that come with the dataset so results are reported in the correct context (e.g., the number of users in the dataset). Naturally, not all datasets in the literature are available in the public domain. The Google Abacus project had collected data from 1500 users over a 6-month period, providing a 27.6 TB dataset, but is not available for public download.

3.5 User Profiles

In a continuous biometric authentication system, the *user profile* contains a digital representation of a user's biometric traits. The user profile is created through the enrolment process, during which features are often extracted from captured biometrics and used to construct a template or classification model. This user profile is used for comparison during the authentication phase by comparing captured biometric samples to the representation in the user profile. This comparison often establishes a similarity score that can be used to decide whether a user is genuine or an impostor. There are a variety of decisions that are needed to form a user profile.

These decisions are related to the biometric traits, the features that may be extracted, the classification approaches, and the potential for fusing multiple biometric traits.

3.5.1 Biometrics

As discussed earlier in Sect. 2.3.3, the term *biometrics* comes from Ancient Greek, with 'bios' meaning 'life' and 'metros' meaning 'to measure' [44]. In the traditional biometric authentication process, a biometric trait is presented to a sensor at the point-of-entry and the user is authenticated. This process can be inconvenient, e.g., requiring a user present their fingerprint onto a scanner. There are often a greater variety of biometrics that may be used within a continuous biometric authentication system than those used in a traditional biometric authentication system (described in Sect. 2.3.3). This is because the biometric traits are collected transparently, allowing for continuous and discrete capture without requiring user interaction. This is not the case in traditional biometric authentication.

The biometric modalities used in continuous biometric authentication systems can differ immensely for different systems. This is due to the wide variety of sensors available on devices (see Sect. 3.3) and the biometric modalities they can provide. There are some *biometric requirements* introduced to assess biometric modalities (see Sect. 4.2) that are useful when comparing different modalities [39]. Some biometrics are selected based on factors such as the performance (e.g., battery or processing power usage) or uniqueness (e.g., ensuring difference between individuals). There are also a variety of other considerations pertaining to context that are considered when a biometric is selected, because authenticating on a biometric from a different context to that the system was trained on may increase error rates [76]. Many continuous biometric authentication systems will also employ multiple biometric modalities to form an authentication score [62]. This approach involves consideration as to how to combine the biometric modalities (e.g., whether the biometric features or the scores for those biometric features are combined).

Biometrics are classed as physiological (describing a physical trait) or behavioural (describing a certain behaviour) [84]. Within these categories exists a plethora of different biometric modalities, each with different advantages and disadvantages. The biometrics employed by continuous biometric authentication systems is vast. For example, touchscreen devices have seen the development of authentication systems that utilise the continuous gesture input as a behavioural biometric to authenticate users [26]. There have been other studies focusing on using the front-facing camera on devices to capture and authenticate physiological facial traits continuously [23]. This section is an overview of how biometrics can be employed in a continuous biometric authentication system. However, a comprehensive overview of biometrics within continuous biometric authentication systems can be found in Chap. 4.

3.5.2 Features

The biometric traits captured by device sensors are usually provided as raw data. Some machine learning techniques for classification can operate solely on this raw data and do not require a feature extraction stage beforehand. However, for other classification techniques it is often required that features are derived from this raw data such that meaningful information can be represented in a common format (i.e., a feature vector) that a classification algorithm can understand. When features are created it can often require some expert knowledge of what may or may not be important about such data (e.g., in touchscreen gesture authentication studies it will be advantageous to know the types of data obtainable via a touchscreen). Sometimes features that are extracted directly from the raw data are known as *base attributes*, whereas features requiring computation are known as *derived attributes* [17].

Obtaining a set of features that can be used to represent the unique characteristics of a biometric trait (or traits) requires a process known as *feature engineering*. This process starts with the feature creation stage (in which expert knowledge of the domain is beneficial). The features decided upon can then be extracted from the raw data and transformed into a common format. An investigation into the features may then be conducted via an exploratory data analysis (EDA), a technique commonly used to find patterns in the features with statistical, correlation, and visualisation techniques. This stage may allow for new insight into the data, such as identifying highly correlated features. The created feature set may then be refined via some feature selection criteria and benchmarking metrics during classification.

There may be other considerations that would need to be considered for some datasets. One of these considerations is missing data, where there may not be data available for the creation of a particular feature. In these cases, it is common to *impute* the missing data with a value derived from a statistical value of the available data in the column (e.g., a mean or median). It may also be the case that there are too many features, which might reduce the classification accuracy or increase the computation time. In these cases, it may be useful to reduce the number of features by removing highly correlated features (e.g., via computing Pearson's correlation coefficient) or removing features with little importance to the classification decision (e.g., via Fisher score ranking).

3.5.3 Classification

Within the context of continuous biometric authentication, classification is generally seen as the process of deciding if some biometric data from a user (stored in a *feature vector*) should be classed as a genuine user or an imposter. Classification is often performed via the application of *machine learning* techniques. Such techniques are a type of artificial intelligence that allow computers to become better at solving problems (i.e., learning) through experience, without explicit programming. The field of machine learning is wide and complex with origins dating back to the 1940s and 1950s. Since then, many machine learning algorithms have been proposed and applied to different problems. Continuous biometric authentication systems have seen wide application of machine learning for classification such that the algorithm can learn the traits of the genuine user (which may not be obvious to a human).

There are a variety of different approaches that can be used depending on the level of human supervision available in the training process. Therefore, machine learning algorithms are commonly grouped as either supervised, unsupervised, semi-supervised, or reinforcement techniques [33]. These techniques are explained below:

- **Supervised**: Supervised learning uses *labelled*[2] data in the training process. Supervised learning can be applied to both *classification* and *regression* problems, though the former is most useful to continuous biometric authentication. Some examples of techniques in this category include k-Nearest Neighbours, Linear Regression, Support Vector Machines (SVMs), and Decision Trees.
- **Unsupervised**: Unsupervised learning techniques are those that utilise unlabelled training data. These have been used in problems such as *clustering* and *anomaly detection*. Some popular algorithms in this category include k-Means, Affinity Propagation, and Local Outlier Factor.
- **Semi-supervised**: This type of learning deals with situations where the data available is partially labelled. The idea is that the labelled data may be used to provide labels for unlabelled data such that a supervised algorithm has more training data and, therefore, greater likelihood of accuracy. This can, in practice, utilise sequential unsupervised and supervised approaches.
- **Reinforcement**: Reinforcement learning is rather different to the previous types of learning. In this system an agent will observe an environment, carry out actions, and receive rewards or penalties as a result. The agent must then learn the best strategy to maximise their reward over time [33]. In 2016, DeepMind's *AlphaGo* used reinforcement learning to create a *Go* champion-beating system.

The most commonly applied learning techniques to continuous biometric authentication systems are supervised algorithms [64]. However, unsupervised anomaly detection algorithms have also been applied in some systems [43]. Typically, supervised learning techniques will perform better than unsupervised learning techniques because they can better model the genuine and imposter users [64]. However, supervised learning assumes that impostor data is available which may not always be the case (e.g., due to privacy). Furthermore, approaches that include an imposter's data in both training and testing may underestimate real-world error rates [22]. Therefore, some studies omit impostors being tested from the training data and use the remaining impostors to model a mock/generalised impostor during training [87].

---

[2] Labelled data is data that is accompanied by the desired or correct solution.

Many machine learning techniques have been applied to continuous biometric authentication systems. In [64], the authors analysed 39 different systems and found that k-Nearest Neighbours, Naive Bayes, Random Forest, and Support Vector Machines were the most used algorithms. The authors in [6] also investigated the field and stated that k-Nearest Neighbours, Support Vector Machines, Artificial Neural Networks, and Decision Trees were commonly used techniques. The following describes a high-level description of how some of these approaches work.

- **Artificial Neural Networks (ANNs)**: These are made up of nodes inspired by neurons in the brain and connections inspired by synapses. There is an input, hidden, and output layer (deep learning approaches contain many hidden layers). Each node represents an activation function and a bias. Connections represent weights that are applied to the source node in the activation function. The weights and biases are initially randomised but iteratively adjusted during training to improve accuracy. They can be accurate but often computationally costly.
- **Support Vector Machines (SVMs)**: SVMs have been widely used because they can provide powerful classification for multi-dimensional data. SVMs work by fitting a maximal margin between samples from separate classes. For problems requiring a nonlinear solution, the kernel trick is applied to better divide classes. These SVMs use hyperparameters C and *gamma* as regularisation parameters that control margin violations and influence of training samples, respectively. Optimal hyperparameters for SVMs are often found using a grid search.
- **Naïve Bayes**: This is a probabilistic classification technique based on the Bayesian theorem and assumes independence between features. Different types of Naïve Bayes classifiers exist for different types of data. These include Multinomial Naïve Bayes, Bernoulli Naïve Bayes, and Gaussian Naïve Bayes. Classifying continuous data often uses a Gaussian distribution (though classification can benefit from Kernel Density Estimation) to compute probabilities. It is a popular algorithm because it is simple to implement and can support high-dimensional data.
- **Random Forest**: Random forests utilise decision trees by forming an ensemble of individual trees [11]. Random forest uses *bagging* where a random sample of the training set is used to build each tree in the forest. Parameters include number of trees and number of leaf nodes. The decision is the class voted for by the majority of trees in the forest. The advantage of random forest is that it can handle high-dimensional data and large datasets, however, the technique operates as a black box and there is little control over the model internals [33].
- ***K*-Nearest Neighbour**: The KNN technique is one of the simplest methods of classification but it is one of the most applied in continuous biometric authentication systems. In the feature space the K represents an integer defining the number of closest neighbours to be considered in the classification of a new sample. The sample is classified as the class of the majority of the neighbours. The distance might be measured using Euclidean distance between features. Choosing an optimal value of K often requires experimentation.

The successful application of these techniques is, as in every application of machine learning, dependent on the quality of the data input into the system. This fact is often referred to as 'garbage in, garbage out' and motivates the use of quality data. Sometimes it is also beneficial to pre-process the data for the benefit of the classifier. This can include scaling features (e.g., between 0 and 1) or reducing the dimensionality of the features (e.g., via Principal Component Analysis (PCA)[3]) to reduce the potential effect of the so-called *curse of dimensionality*. The detrimental effects of *overfitting* (where algorithms model noise in the data) or *underfitting* (where an algorithm cannot effectively model the data) should also be considered.

Each of these machine learning algorithms might further be used in an architecture known as *ensemble learning*. These architectures attempt to improve the accuracy obtained via individual classifiers by aggregating multiple classifiers [33]. The key methods to do this include *bagging*, *boosting*, and *stacking*.[4] There are, of course, a whole field of techniques and considerations that have been explored and applied to continuous biometric authentication systems (including newer techniques such as *federated learning* [55]) but which go beyond the scope of this summary.

3.5.4   Biometric Fusion

In the book by James Surowiecki entitled *The Wisdom of Crowds*, it is described how groups can (though not always) form better decisions than individuals alone [81]. This is similar in biometric authentication systems. It has been shown in multiple studies that the fusion of multiple sources of biometric information (whether it be multiple biometric traits or instances of the same trait) can lead to increased accuracies and lower error rates, as well as robustness against attacks [77].

Thus far the biometrics discussed have been described as being a single source of evidence. There are other ways to employ biometrics to produce *multiple* sources of evidence. These approaches are known as *multibiometrics* and employ these sources of evidence via different strategies. The advantage of multibiometrics is that the additional evidence can lead to higher levels of recognition accuracy and make attacks more difficult [62]. Multibiometrics has not yet seen significant adoption in industry. The adoption rate stood at around 15% in 2021, largely due to the impressive accuracies of the currently used one-shot traits such as fingerprints, faces, and irises, which had adoption rates of 40%, 15%, and 13%, respectively [37]. However, some of these high accuracy biometrics do not lend themselves well to continuous authentication systems. Such systems often employ lower accuracy (but continuous) biometrics which can benefit from multibiometrics. The categories

---

[3] PCA projects a high dimensionality feature set to a lower dimensional space by representing correlated features into single features to maximise the variance of data in the resulting feature set.

[4] More information on these ensemble learning techniques can be found in [33].

of multibiometrics commonly described in the literature are as follows [62]:

- **Multi-sensor**: In this type of biometric system only one biometric is collected, but it is collected from multiple sensors such that even more information can be obtained from that single biometric. One example of this might be obtaining a face from a thermal infrared camera *and* a visible light camera, which can enhance the accuracy [79]. The additional information can increase the accuracy of the system but the additional sensors may incur costs [62].
- **Multi-modal**: This approach utilises and combines multiple biometric modalities. This is advantageous because it means an attacker would have to successfully spoof multiple biometrics to access the system. This type of system can use two or more modalities. The approach in [77] combined scores from touchscreen gestures *and* faces. They showed increased accuracy and robustness against attacks in which only one biometric was spoofed.
- **Multi-algorithm**: This type of multibiometric system uses multiple algorithms to process the same captured biometric. This can entail different algorithms for the extraction of multiple feature sets or different classification algorithms applied to the same biometric trait [62]. An example of this is the extraction of multiple facial features from a single face image, such as in [65] where LBP and attribute feature vectors are produced to form a combined score.
- **Multi-instance**: Systems employing multi-instance (also known as *multi-unit*) biometrics capture different instances of the same biometric trait, such as left iris and right iris. One use case for multi-instance biometrics is in law enforcement, where it is common to take the fingerprints of all ten fingers [62]. Because the same trait is being collected, it may not be necessary to use multiple sensors.
- **Multi-sample**: In a multi-sample approach, a single sensor is used to collect multiple different samples of the same biometric. Systems employing faces for biometric authentication might capture a face from multiple different angles such that a more detailed representation of a user's face can be captured [62]. This can improve the accuracy of a biometric system within requiring additional sensors but may be inconvenient for users to provide multiple samples.

Recent continuous authentication works have shown considerable benefits in producing multi-modal systems. These take advantage of the sensor-dense user devices that have developed since the early 2010s, allowing for multiple biometric modalities to be collected. However, the use of multi-modal biometrics in continuous authentication schemes is still relatively new. In a 2016 study it was noted that in their survey of continuous authentication systems that only 30% of the schemes employed multi-modal biometrics [3]. The advantages of multi-modal biometrics are numerous. Compared with *uni-modal* systems, multi-modal biometric systems can expect better protection from spoof attacks, higher recognition rates, less affected by environmental factors, and increased robustness and reliability [64]. There are various levels in the authentication process that biometric information can be fused and a variety of techniques to do it. The three levels at which fusion commonly occurs (feature level, score level, and decision level) are discussed below.

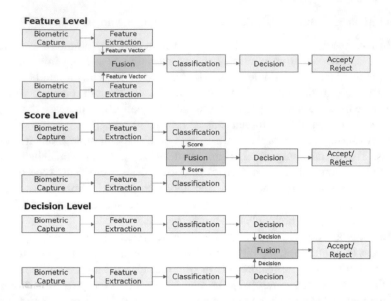

Fig. 3.2 The three levels at which biometrics are commonly fused within a biometric authentication architecture (adapted from [61])

Figure 3.2 illustrates where these levels are located in a continuous authentication system.

- **Feature Level**: Fusing biometrics at the feature level sees the fusion occur at the point at which the biometric features are extracted. Given several independent biometric feature vectors consisting of measurements of the same scale, the fusion process will fuse these feature vectors into a single higher dimensionality feature vector [61]. This fused feature vector can contain a greater amount of identifying information than the original feature vectors [38], providing biometrics are of sufficient quality. One caveat of this approach is that higher dimensionality feature vectors can suffer from the *curse of dimensionality*, hindering classification.
- **Score Level**: The score level fusion approach combines the individual scores that are obtained from the classification of biometric modalities. When fusing scores from different classifiers it is sometimes the case that scores will be heterogeneous and not homogenous. If such heterogeneous scores were fused the meaning may be lost due to the different score ranges. The method used to solve this issue is known as *normalisation*, and it maps scores to the same range before they are fused. The normalisation techniques commonly used include:
  - **tanh-estimator**: Given that μ_G and σ_G are the mean and standard deviations of genuine scores, the normalised score s_i' is

$$s_i' = \frac{1}{2} \left\{ \tanh \left(0.01 \times \left(\frac{scr_i - \mu_G}{\sigma_G} \right) \right) + 1 \right\} \qquad (3.1)$$

- **min-max**: To convert a score s_i to a normalised score s_i' using the maximum (*max*) and minimum (*min*) scores is given by

$$s_i' = \frac{s_i - \min}{\max - \min} \tag{3.2}$$

- **z-score**: The z-score normalisation technique is equated for a score s_i using the mean (μ) and standard deviation (σ) by

$$s_i' = \frac{s_i - \mu}{\sigma} \tag{3.3}$$

After scores have been normalised to a common range, the fusion of the scores can occur. There are multiple methods to do this. Some of the most common techniques include the following (with an optional weighting variable (w_i)):

- **Sum Rule**: The sum rule is simply the total of all scores from all classifiers:

$$score = \sum_{i=1}^{n} w_i s_i \tag{3.4}$$

- **Product Rule**: In the product rule all of the scores are multiplied together:

$$score = \prod_{i=1}^{n} w_i s_i \tag{3.5}$$

- **Minimum Rule**: The minimum rule takes the minimum score of all scores.

$$score = \min(w_1 s_1, w_2 s_2, w_3 s_3, \ldots, w_i s_i) \tag{3.6}$$

- **Maximum Rule**: The maximum rule takes the maximum score of all scores.

$$score = \max(w_1 s_1, w_2 s_2, w_3 s_3, \ldots, w_i s_i) \tag{3.7}$$

- **Decision Level**: In decision-level fusion the decision (e.g., genuine or not genuine user) from each individual classifier is used to produce an overall decision. Such techniques at this level may include majority voting (in which the majority decision forms the overall decision) and the AND and OR rules [36].

The preferred practice is to fuse the multi-modal biometrics at the score level [34]. This level does not have the rigidity of decision-level fusion and is not affected by potential feature incompatibilities of extraction level fusion [36]. Multi-modal approaches perform better when the modalities are uncorrelated compared to when there is correlation [62]. Another consideration for continuous authentication is the temporal nature of the modalities, because it is possible some can be collected more frequently than others and multiple modalities may not always be available [72].

3.6   Evaluation

The evaluation stage refers to the process of gaining insight as to how effective the continuous biometric authentication system is. This process is usually carried out after a system has been constructed, trained, and is able to produce scores on the biometrics captured. To gauge the effectiveness of the system at differentiating between genuine and impostor users, there are often be thresholds set that scores can be compared to. After one or more thresholds have been set to decide on what score is needed to confer or deny access to certain resources, some metrics indicative of the number of false acceptances or false rejections can be calculated. The decision on what should be done if a score (or multiple scores) drop below a certain threshold can vary in different systems (see Sect. 3.6.3). The practical assessment of a system is usually done within experimental settings, and additional metrics (such as robustness to attack and resource consumption) are sometimes considered.

3.6.1   Threshold Selection

The score obtained from classifying a biometric sample is often a probabilistic value representing the similarity of the sample to the biometrics the system was trained on. Therefore, biometric scores are not binary and will instead occupy a value within a certain range (e.g., between 0% and 100%). Therefore, a value needs to be selected to determine whether a biometric sample is categorised as that of a genuine user or an imposter. This value is known as the *threshold*. Scores obtained from the biometric sample need to equal or surpass the threshold to be authenticated as the genuine user (assuming higher scores imply increased likelihood of the genuine user). This is formalised as a two-class classification problem in which a claimed identity I and a biometric sample x_n that has produced a score s when compared to user profile x_I is categorised by a threshold thr [39]. This is defined as below in Eq. (3.8):

$$(I, x_n) \in \begin{cases} genuine & \text{if } s \geq thr \\ impostor & \text{if } s < thr \end{cases} \tag{3.8}$$

The selection of an appropriate threshold is crucial to the security and usability of a continuous authentication system. High thresholds can decrease the false

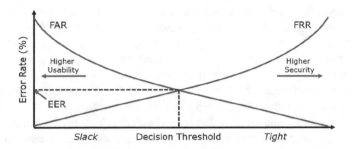

Fig. 3.3 Showing the compromise between usability and security; higher thresholds increase FRR (false rejection rate), whereas lower threshold increase the FAR (false acceptance rate)

acceptance of impostors but can also increase the false rejection of genuine users. Low thresholds can decrease the false rejection of genuine users but can also increase the false acceptance of impostors. In the literature it is common to set the threshold at the point of the equal error rate (where the rate of false acceptance and false rejection are equal) because this provides a simple metric to compare different systems. In practice, the selection of a threshold is a compromise between the security and the usability [78]. This concept is visualised in Fig. 3.3.

In cases of high security thresholds may be increased to reduce false acceptance and in cases of high usability thresholds may be decreased to reduce false rejection. This compromise is seen in current biometric authentication systems. The recommended security measures for strong biometric authentication on Android devices expect that the false acceptance rate would be 0.002% and the false rejection rate would be 10%.[5] Similarly, the FIDO Alliance has a requirement for certification that no more than 3% of attempts by the genuine user should be falsely rejected and no more than 0.01% of attempts by an impostor should be falsely accepted.[6] In these cases, the threshold is set with a preference for security. However, continuous authentication schemes assess biometrics frequently and, therefore, have multiple attempts at detecting impostors, and in such systems it may be prudent to set a threshold favouring usability (as even with false acceptance rates of 10% it becomes an increasingly small probability an impostor would evade detection for a long period).

There are two ways a threshold can be implemented. The first is as a *global* [50] (also known as *system-wide* [14]) threshold. Global thresholds are the same for all users of the system. The benefit of this is that thresholds are selected once and are applied quickly to new users. However, global thresholds are generalised for the average user and lack individuality [14]. The second type of threshold is

---

[5] https://source.android.com/security/biometric/measure.

[6] https://fidoalliance.org/specs/biometric/Biometrics-Requirements-v1.0-wd-20190606.html# Requirements.

person-based [50] (also known as *individual* [14]). The benefit of this is that it is calibrated and unique for each user. However, they require computation to identify each user's appropriate threshold. In [50] the authors found a person-based threshold outperformed the global threshold for mouse movement biometrics.

Thresholds employed in continuous authentication schemes are often a fixed value and do not change. These can be considered *fixed* thresholds. However, they assume the same threshold is required in all circumstances, which is unrealistic and may impact usability and security. Some recent studies have performed experiments on *adaptive* thresholds. In [88] the authors proposed adapting the threshold based on an exponentially weighted moving average (EWMA) of a prior window of scores such that the threshold stays similar to the current scores expected but identifies significant deviations. In [78] a system is developed that adapts the threshold for touchscreen gestures based on the trust in passively collected sensor data. Utilising the trust in the passively collected sensor data to adapt the threshold halved the false acceptance and false rejection rates compared to a static threshold. These studies indicate adaptive thresholds have the potential to yield benefits to security and usability.

3.6.2 Metrics

Continuous authentication systems are in essence a two-class classification problem in which the scores obtained from a user's biometrics are categorised into either the genuine or impostor class. This creates four possible outcomes for the system. If the user is genuine, then the outcome may be a *true acceptance* or a *false rejection* (also known as a *type 1 error*). Conversely, if the user is an impostor, then the outcome may be a *true rejection* or a *false acceptance* (also known as a *type 2 error*). These four outcomes are represented in Table 3.2. The optimal continuous authentication system will minimise the occurrence of both false rejection and false acceptance.

There are several metrics used to assess the performance of a continuous authentication system, based on the outcomes in Table 3.2, that are common in biometric authentication literature. The fundamental measures of the accuracy of a biometric system are the *False Non-Match Rate* (FNMR) and the *False Match Rate* (FMR). Respectively, these metrics are often referred to as the *False Rejection*

Table 3.2 The evaluation matrix for a biometric reading, showing that biometric decisions can be classified into one of the four categories

		Predicted class	
		Genuine	Impostor
Actual class	Genuine	True Accept	False Reject
	Impostor	False Accept	True Reject

Rate (FRR) and *False Acceptance Rate* (FAR)[7] within the context of biometric authentication [39]. Related to the FRR and FAR are the rates that the user is correctly categorised. These metrics are the *True Rejection Rate* (TRR) and the *True Acceptance Rate* (TAR) (also known as the *Genuine Accept Rate* (GAR) and sometimes used as an alternative to reporting the FRR [39]). These metrics can be computed via the following:

- **False Rejection Rate (FRR):** This is the rate at which a genuine user is falsely rejected by the system as an impostor. Lower rates indicate better performance.

$$FAR = \frac{\#\ Rejected\ Genuine\ Biometrics}{\#\ Total\ Genuine\ Biometrics} \tag{3.9}$$

- **False Acceptance Rate (FAR):** This is the rate at which an impostor is falsely accepted by the system as the genuine user. Lower rates indicate better performance.

$$FAR = \frac{\#\ Accepted\ Impostor\ Biometrics}{\#\ Total\ Impostor\ Biometrics} \tag{3.10}$$

- **True Rejection Rate (TRR):** This is the rate at which impostors are correctly rejected by the system. Higher rates indicate better performance.

$$TRR = \frac{\#\ Rejected\ Impostor\ Biometrics}{\#\ Total\ Impostor\ Biometrics} \tag{3.11}$$

- **True Acceptance Rate (TAR):** This is the rate at which genuine users are correctly accepted by the system. Higher rates indicate better performance.

$$TAR = \frac{\#\ Accepted\ Genuine\ Biometrics}{\#\ Total\ Genuine\ Biometrics} \tag{3.12}$$

Some of these metrics are related. Obtaining either the FRR or the TAR allows the other to be derived; FRR can be obtained via $1 - TAR$ and TAR can be obtained via $1 - FRR$. Similarly, obtaining either the FAR or the TRR allows the other to be derived; TRR can be obtained via $1 - FAR$ and FAR can be obtained via $1 - TRR$.

The FAR and the FRR are dependent on the threshold set to determine whether a score is classified as the genuine user or as an impostor. Because different thresholds for different systems can vary the FAR and FRR it can sometimes be difficult to

---

[7] Whilst FRR and FAR are often used synonymously for FNMR and FMR, respectively, they are not always identical. FNMR and FMR refer to performance at the matching level only. FRR and FAR refer to performance from system decisions and may, therefore, include false acceptance/rejection due to system errors (e.g., failure to acquire) [46]. However, here they are treated as synonymous.

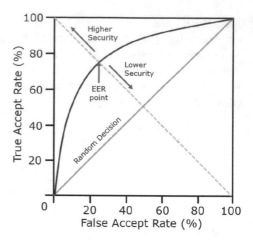

Fig. 3.4 An ROC (Receiver Operating Characteristic) curve plots a curve and can be used to assess the performance of a binary classifier system at different thresholds

compare the FAR and FRR. The third error rate that is commonly presented for a biometric authentication system is the *Equal Error Rate* (EER). The EER is the point at which the selected thresholds yields an equal FAR and FRR. This makes an appropriate measurement for performance of biometric authentication systems because it creates a standardised and comparable metric.

- **Equal Error Rate (EER)**: This is the error rate at which the FAR is equal to the FRR as the authentication threshold is varied (this point of EER is commonly visualised in an ROC curve, seen in Fig. 3.4). Given a finite number of genuine and impostor scores with adequate granularity, the FAR and FRR values with the smallest distance can be averaged [84]. Therefore, EER can be computed as follows for the FAR and FRR with the smallest difference:

$$EER = \frac{FAR + FRR}{2} \tag{3.13}$$

Whilst the above metrics are the most common to biometric authentication systems [64], other metrics have also been used and proposed. One of these is *accuracy*. This is a metric which computes the total portion of the test data that was correctly classified. Therefore, it should be noted that accuracy does not give the nuanced information as to what portion of the correctly/incorrectly classified users were genuine or impostors. Given the number or true acceptances (TA) and true rejections (TR), accuracy can be computed as the portion these represent of all tested samples (including the false acceptances (FA) and false rejections (FR)):

$$Accuracy = \frac{\#TA + \#TR}{\#TA + \#TR + \#FA + \#FR} \tag{3.14}$$

Some have argued that the metrics discussed thus far are not optimal to evaluate continuous biometric authentication systems and urge the use of metrics specifically designed for the nuances of such systems. In [10], the authors present the metrics *average number of impostor actions* (ANIA) and *average number of genuine actions* (ANGA). The authors claim these metrics place emphasis on *when* an impostor is detected instead of *if* they are detected. The ANIA represents the average number of actions an impostor can do before they are correctly detected and the ANGA represents the average number of actions a genuine user can do before they are falsely rejected. Ideally, ANIA should be as low as possible and ANGA should be as high as possible. These metrics, however, are not (as yet) widely adopted.

There are some important considerations for the FAR, FRR, and EER metrics. In [22] the authors use Gini coefficients to analyse the distribution of the error rates to determine if errors are *random* or *systemic* among users. This is because a FAR of 20% may imply that all attackers are detected 80% of the time *or* it may mean that 20% of attackers are *never* detected and 80% are detected immediately. This is illustrated in Fig. 3.5. It follows that biometric systems may not be equally discriminative for all users. Some users within a biometric system may suffer from high inter-class similarity (e.g., faces of the young are less distinguishable than those of adults) and, therefore, have higher false acceptance rates. Users have been characterised in some literature according to a 1998 work [19], popularly known as *Doddington's zoo*, in which users are divided into four categories based on the way the system reacts to their biometrics. These user categories are:

- **Sheep**: The sheep are those that hold biometric traits that are distinct with high intra-class similarity (resulting in low FARs and FRRs).
- **Goats**: These are users that have high intra-class variation. This results in members of this group having relatively a high FRR.
- **Lambs**: The lambs are users that have biometrics that have a high degree of overlap with other users (high inter-class similarity). The FARs associated with these users are, therefore, typically high [39].
- **Wolves**: These are a category of user that deliberately manipulate their biometric traits (more so with behavioural traits) to impersonate another user [39]. These users perform adversary attacks and can increase the FAR of the system.

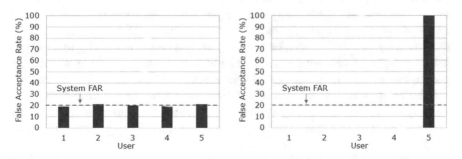

Fig. 3.5 Showing possible FAR distributions when a single attacker impersonates different users (as discussed in [22]). On the left are *random* errors (leading to eventual detection) and on the right is a *systematic* error (with no eventual detection). The dotted line denotes the reported 20% FAR of both samples. These distributions among users can lead to security and evaluation challenges

The evaluation of FARs and FRRs for a continuous biometric authentication system may not necessitate a preference toward security over usability. This is because (unlike traditional point-of-entry biometric authentication) the authentication is not carried out once but frequently. Therefore, a system performing face recognition with a FRR of 2% may, on average, only falsely reject a genuine user once every 50 authentication attempts, which may not degrade user experience if used to authenticate at the point-of-entry only but may severely impact usability if performed continuously. Conversely, as discussed in Sect. 3.6.1, even larger FARs offer security because continuous assessments increase the likelihood of detection over time.

The metrics discussed thus far represent the ability of the continuous biometric authentication system to discern genuine users from impostors. However, there are other metrics to measure other aspects of the system that might be used in an evaluation. One is the *failure to acquire* (FTA) rate. This rate is the portion of authentication attempts in which the biometric sensor cannot capture the required sample [39]. Another common metric is the *failure to enrol* (FTE) rate, which is the portion of users that cannot be successfully enrolled within the system [39].

3.6.3   Decision

Traditional biometric authentication grants or denies access to a device or system by comparing a score from a biometric against a threshold. Similarly, most discussion on continuous biometric authentication systems assume that they will grant (or maintain) access so long as scores from continuously collected biometric samples do not drop below a threshold. However, some recently developed systems refine this paradigm and do not always revoke access at the first score below a certain threshold. Such systems take a more nuanced approach to forming a decision on the appropriate action to implement when scores are above or below a certain threshold. In practice this can produce more usable systems with a risk-based approach.

Some systems will form a decision on what action to take based on a window of sensor samples instead of simply one sample. There are benefits to this in cases where the quality of a certain biometric trait is known to be variable between immediate samples. This can be seen in [26], where a system employing touchscreen gestures experimented with different numbers of gestures to form a decision, eventually utilising 13 gestures to achieve a reported 0% EER. Using multiple samples might utilise some biometric fusion techniques discussed in Sect. 3.5.4. This type of approach usually requires a succession of multiple poorly matching biometric samples in a row to revoke access rather than a single poorly matching sample.

It should also be mentioned that there are several systems that do not make a binary access decision based on the whether one or more biometric samples exceed a threshold but instead implement different actions or policies based on the score. This can result in the revocation of certain privileges or permissions as the score obtained from the samples reduces. This approach can be seen in [60] where a *progressive authentication* system is proposed using multiple biometric traits to produce a score that informed which applications a user should have access to. This approach fits into the recommendations from the UK's NCSC which advises risk-based authentication and access control.[8] Another type of system may use a *dynamic trust model*; this is done in [51] where the system will have a global trust score that is increased or decreased based on the score from collected touchscreen gestures.

3.6.4 Assessment Process

The practical assessment of any system is a necessity before it is deployed in the real-world so performance metrics (and possibly other factors) can be evaluated against the needs of an application [56]. To assess a continuous biometric authentication system, as with a regular point-of-entry biometric system, it is first enrolled on the genuine user's biometrics (and possibly those of the impostor users if a two-class classification technique is used) to form their user profile. In practice, this assessment is initially done in an experimental setting in which a researcher will have a dataset of pre-collected user biometrics at hand (such as those discussed in Sect. 3.4.2) to evaluate different experimental variables (e.g., classification algorithms).

To produce the performance metrics in Sect. 3.6.2, the researcher will then (after enrolment is complete) gather the output scores when the system is tested on the data of genuine and impostor users (to ensure that it can discriminate between the two). It is important that the test biometrics are a section of the dataset that was not involved in the enrolment phase (otherwise this system is only being tested on the ability to tune itself to a particular dataset) [56]. The testing is often done through k-fold cross validation, in which k experiments are run and a different $\frac{1}{k}$ of the data (a fold) is used for testing. Then through applying a threshold to the scores (with the considerations discussed in Sect. 3.6.1) the researcher can produce metrics, such as the FAR, FRR, and EER values. These metrics can be used to assess if the system is suitable for further experimentation/deployment. However, there may be different levels of performance required for different applications and purposes [56].

Whilst the metrics discussed in Sect. 3.6.2 are a common form of assessment, other factors are also important and have been considered [64]. The chosen biometrics can be assessed according to the biometric requirements (explored in Sect. 4.2) [39], such as acceptability. Robustness toward spoof attacks (and other threats in Sect. 3.8) is also of growing importance. Timings are also often considered, such as the time to extract features and authenticate a user. The consumption of device resources (such as processing, memory, storage, and battery) can all be a

---

[8] https://www.ncsc.gov.uk/collection/device-security-guidance/bring-your-own-device/action-3-understand-additional-costs-and-implications.

consideration in deciding on an approach. All of the metrics and measurements discussed require compromise (e.g., some algorithms may be more prone to error but require fewer resources); no solution will give optimal values for each metric and researchers must make appropriate compromises for the application.

3.7   User Perceptions

Whilst there are issues with existing authentication mechanisms, they are nonetheless broadly accepted by users. Continuous authentication systems relying on biometrics have different requirements to traditional mechanisms (e.g., the password) and instead require continual samples of biometrics to authenticate during usage sessions. It is, therefore, important that users see these systems as trustworthy, reliable, and effective such that overall perception is positive. This can ensure that the solutions being developed in academia and industry would be adopted by users.

There have been various studies to gauge user opinions of continuous authentication. In [15] the authors perform a study with 27 users trialling a continuous authentication system (utilising face, voice, and keystroke biometrics) and subsequently surveying their experience. The results showed that 92% of users found the system more secure than traditional forms of authentication. It was also found that 81% of users would use such a scheme in practice, the remaining 19% stated that whilst the system offered increased security they did not need increased security on their device. Lastly, 86% stated they found the scheme to be secure or very secure.

In [16], the authors assessed the opinions of 30 volunteers performing tasks that required different levels of security on an *iPhone 4*. The users were told a transparent authentication score would be computed based on their voice and keystroke biometrics which would determine a level of device trust. When surveyed the users felt the continuous authentication solution provided a sense of security (with most agreeing it felt at *least* as secure as their current authentication mechanism). However, users did cite inconvenience when falsely rejected by the system. Overall, the perception was positive with 90% of users stating they would consider using such a system.

In [2], the researchers explored 302 users' perceptions surrounding the collection of usage behaviour and found that 58% of users would accept a system using monitoring their behaviour, 16% of users would reject the system, and 26% were neutral. Interestingly, they also found that 57% of users preferred their biometric templates stayed on the device (only 26% would prefer they were stored with a trusted third party). A survey in [41] explored the perceptions of 37 users. They found continuous authentication was found convenient by 91% of users (only 65% said the same for explicit techniques, such as PINs). The study also found such systems are seen as secure with 81% of users indicating it provides satisfactory protection. The results revealed 63% of users would use continuous authentication (33% wanting it as their primary authentication mechanism and 30% using it as a secondary mechanism).

In [59] the authors surveyed 500 users and found over 60% found continuous authentication convenient (only 10% found it inconvenient). Furthermore, 65% of users found it had greater security than traditional authentication. Overall, 46.6% of the users stated they would use continuous authentication (due to the convenience) whilst 33.4% may use it and 20% would not. In [75] the researchers conduct a survey on 778 users on their views on behavioural continuous authentication systems and found 72.4% of users had the intention to use such systems. Their results did suggest those with privacy concerns may worry about misuse of biometrics, motivating reliability and trustworthiness in system implementation.

3.8 Threats

Authentication is one of the most important lines of defence in preventing access to a computer system (or resources on that system) by unauthorised users. It is for this reason that authentication mechanisms are under threat from attackers. Ever since authentication mechanisms were implemented on computer systems, there have been consistent threats from those wishing to bypass them. These threats manifest in different ways for different authentication systems. For example, knowledge-based authentication has threats such as shoulder-surfing and brute force attacks, whereas token-based authentication carries risk of token theft. There are also different types of attackers, with different knowledge and resources at their disposal.

There can be considered two primary classes of attackers. These are described as *informed* and *uninformed* attackers [40]. Uninformed attackers have very little or no prior knowledge about the user (e.g., what they look like or their behaviour). This can be thought of as an attacker who finds or steals a device and attempts to gain access, such as a theft of a mobile device by a thief on a moped (as has been prevalent on London streets). Many uninformed attackers will perform *zero-effort* attacks in which the attacker simply presents their biometric to the system to gain access. This makes them relatively simple to detect due to biometric mismatch (and, therefore, have been said to be an unrealistic attack scenario). However, there is the possibility an uninformed attacker uses statistical techniques to mimic a *typical* user, which can still increase keyboard EERs by between 28.6% and 84.4% [66].

An informed attacker poses a greater threat to a system as they have prior knowledge about the user. They may know or have access to some of the genuine user's biometrics, such as their behavioural information. This knowledge allows informed attackers to perform *active* attacks such as *presentation attacks*[9] via a spoofed biometric (for physiological biometrics) or an *imitation attack* (for behavioural biometrics) [21]. Utilising this user knowledge in their attack can

---

[9] Defined by the recent ISO/IEC 30107 standard, presentation attacks are a 'presentation to the biometric capture subsystem with the goal of interfering with the operation of the biometric system'.

increase their likelihood of gaining access to the system. Informed attackers in [40] with knowledge of the users day-to-day application and location habits were detected less than their uninformed counterparts when they imitated the genuine user behaviour. However, these types of attack require effort from the attacker in that they may have to obtain a biometric or knowledge of it and use it to circumvent the authentication system.

Some attackers may obtain a digital representation of a user's biometric trait to perform attacks. Some physiological biometrics such as faces are easily obtainable via social media and can be used to circumvent systems relying on facial biometrics [29]. Behavioural biometrics such as touchscreen gestures have also been forged, using a $400 Lego robot, by attackers that obtained samples of the genuine biometric (increasing the FAR fivefold) [67]. Furthermore, effective forgeries of motion biometrics obtained via screen taps have been produced via generative adversarial network (GAN) approaches [57]. However, many of these attacks require a motivated attacker with considerable information and possibly finance behind them.

The threats discussed thus far have focused on attacks at the biometric sensor but there are other threats that target other system components [53]. The various threats and the components at which they occur at are shown in Fig. 3.6 and briefly described here. Replay attacks can bypass the sensing module and replay a previously intercepted biometric. Overriding the feature extractor can allow attackers to produce features of their choosing. Attacks synthesising a feature vector replace the features with those of the attacker. Overriding the matcher or final decision involves an attacker modifying these elements of the system to produce erroneous output. Modifying the template of the system can see attackers replace stored biometric information with their own. Channel interception might see an attacker load in their information when biometric information is passed to the matching algorithm.

Some of these threats require specialist skills, hardware or capabilities and do not always come from lone individuals. There are different types of actor that may attempt to circumvent the system, each with different levels of experience and resources. Those that pose a threat to circumventing computer system security have before been categorised into types including spies, crooks, researchers, and bullies

Fig. 3.6 There are a variety of points in any biometric system in which an attack might be carried out in the system. The diagram has been adapted from that in [82]

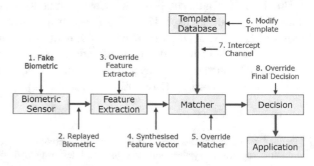

[5]. These threat actors may not all necessarily be acting maliciously though; in 2016 researchers at Michigan State University helped police in a homicide investigation by unlocking a smartphone via a 2D printed fingerprint [13]. It is worth noting that particularly unscrupulous threat actors may bypass the discussed attack vectors and use coercive tactics to force the genuine user to grant them access [47].

3.9   Use Cases

There are, of course, a plethora of use cases for continuous authentication systems. Such a system can offer greater protection to any modern device that has sensors from which biometrics can be continuously (or frequently) gathered and processed. This makes it a desirable solution for any person or organisation wishing to enhance the security of their system whilst maintaining usability. This section briefly describes several of the prominent use cases that could benefit from the deployment of continuous authentication systems, but it is by no means an exhaustive list.

One obvious application for continuous authentication is for organisations that need to provide secure and usable security solutions for their systems. This might be deployed by a business that manages employee or customer devices (or allows for bring-your-own-device (BYOD)) to protect against attacks or fraud. Government organisations will also find benefit to the deployment of continuous authentication systems on their devices, as it can help keep information on devices protected. This is pertinent considering that within 12 months the UK Government lost 2004 devices, including smartphones, laptops, and tablets [8]. There are military use cases for continuous authentication, to secure the communications devices used by soldiers in situations where devices may be lost or stolen by the enemy [12].

One field that can benefit from not only the additional security of continuous authentication but also the usability is healthcare. It has been reported that healthcare professionals must perform a range of different login procedures for a variety of different healthcare systems. In 2020, the BBC described how some staff within the UK's National Health Service were required to login to up to 15 different computer systems a day (with 1 minute 45 seconds spent logging in) [7]. This kind of login slows down the service provided to patients and may consequently impact the level of care provided. It has been suggested that utilising continuous authentication approaches on devices used by medical professionals could enhance the healthcare process by removing the need to explicitly authenticate, thus saving time [30].

Continuous authentication systems are also applicable within educational institutions to authenticate students and replace non-scalable human invigilation. This has been noted as a particularly useful tool for distance learning [25] and would allow students to be verified whilst they take courses and exams remotely (such as was required for many during the Covid-19 pandemic). In [24], a continuous student authentication system for e-learning platforms is proposed through utilising face, voice, touch, mouse, and keystroke biometrics. The study describes the system being able to attest student identity throughout the learning experience.

3.10 Summary

This chapter explored the concept, architecture, and components of a continuous biometric authentication system. The motivations behind creating continuous biometric authentication systems were first discussed. Then the concept was defined and the architecture was presented. The user devices and the built-in sensing capabilities that enable this type of authentication were then described. Next, some datasets that might be used for experimentation were provided and the creation of user profiles (including classification and biometric fusion) was discussed. The way that these types of systems are usually evaluated was then shown. Then studies showing the user perceptions of such systems were surveyed. Lastly, some threats to such systems were discussed and as were potential use cases for such systems.

References

1. Abuhamad, M., Abusnaina, A., Nyang, D., Mohaisen, D.: Sensor-based continuous authentication of smartphones' users using behavioral biometrics: a contemporary survey. IEEE Internet Things J. **8**(1), 65–84 (2021)
2. Al Abdulwahid, A., Clarke, N., Stengel, I., Furnell, S., Reich, C.: Security, privacy and usability—a survey of users' perceptions and attitudes. In: Fischer-Hübner, S., Lambrinoudakis, C., López, J. (eds.) Trust, Privacy and Security in Digital Business, pp. 153–168. Springer International Publishing, Cham (2015)
3. Al Abdulwahid, A., Clarke, N., Stengel, I., Furnell, S., Reich, C.: Continuous and transparent multimodal authentication: reviewing the state of the art. Clust. Comput. **19**(1), 455–474 (2016)
4. Al Solami, E., Boyd, C., Clark, A., Islam, A.K.: Continuous biometric authentication: can it be more practical? In: 2010 IEEE 12th International Conference on High Performance Computing and Communications (HPCC), pp. 647–652 (2010)
5. Anderson, R.J.: Security Engineering: A Guide to Building Dependable Distributed Systems, 3rd edn. Wiley Publishing, New York (2021)
6. Baig, A.F., Eskeland, S.: Security, privacy, and usability in continuous authentication: a survey. Sensors **21**(17), 5967 (2021)
7. BBC: 'outdated' it leaves NHS staff with 15 different computer logins. https://www.bbc.co.uk/news/health-50972123
8. BBC: Thousands of mobiles and laptops lost by UK government in a year. https://www.bbc.co.uk/news/technology-51572578
9. Beguin, E., Besnard, S., Cros, A., Joannes, B., Leclerc-Istria, O., Noel, A., Roels, N., Taleb, F., Thongphan, J., Alata, E., Nicomette, V.: Computer-security-oriented escape room. IEEE Secur. Priv. **17**(4), 78–83 (2019)
10. Bours, P., Mondal, S.: Performance evaluation of continuous authentication systems. IET Biom. **4**, 220–226(6) (2015)
11. Breiman, L.: Random forests. Mach. Learn. **45**(1), 5–32 (2001)
12. Brown, J.D., Pase, W., McKenzie, C., Salmanian, M., Tang, H.: A prototype implementation of continuous authentication for tactical applications. In: Zhou, Y., Kunz, T. (eds.) Ad Hoc Networks, pp. 342–353. Springer International Publishing, Cham (2017)
13. Chugh, T., Jain, A.K.: Fingerprint presentation attack detection: generalization and efficiency. In: 2019 International Conference on Biometrics (ICB), pp. 1–8 (2019)
14. Clarke, N.: Transparent User Authentication: Biometrics, RFID and Behavioural Profiling, 1st edn. Springer Publishing Company, Inc., Berlin (2011)

15. Clarke, N., Karatzouni, S., Furnell, S.: Flexible and transparent user authentication for mobile devices. In: Gritzalis, D., Lopez, J. (eds.) Emerging Challenges for Security, Privacy and Trust, pp. 1–12. Springer, Berlin (2009)
16. Crawford, H., Renaud, K.: Understanding user perceptions of transparent authentication on a mobile device. Journal of Trust Management 1(1), 7 (2014)
17. Dasgupta, D., Roy, A., Nag, A.: Advances in User Authentication, 1st edn. Springer Publishing Company, Incorporated, New York (2017)
18. De Luca, A., Hang, A., von Zezschwitz, E., Hussmann, H.: I feel like I'm taking selfies all day! towards understanding biometric authentication on smartphones. In: Proceedings of the 33rd Annual ACM Conference on Human Factors in Computing Systems, CHI '15, pp. 1411–1414. Association for Computing Machinery, New York (2015)
19. Doddington, G., Liggett, W., Martin, A., Przybocki, M., Reynolds, D.: SHEEP, GOATS, LAMBS and WOLVES: a statistical analysis of speaker performance in the NIST 1998 speaker recognition evaluation. Tech. rep., National Institute of Standards and Technology Gaithersburg, MD (1998)
20. Eagle, N., (Sandy) Pentland, A.: Reality mining: sensing complex social systems. Pers. Ubiquit. Comput. 10(4), 255–268 (2006)
21. Eberz, S.: Security Analysis of Behavioural Biometrics for Continuous Authentication. Ph.D. thesis, University of Oxford, Oxford (2018)
22. Eberz, S., Rasmussen, K.B., Lenders, V., Martinovic, I.: Evaluating behavioral biometrics for continuous authentication: challenges and metrics. In: Proceedings of the 2017 ACM on Asia Conference on Computer and Communications Security, ASIA CCS '17, pp. 386–399. Association for Computing Machinery, New York (2017)
23. Fathy, M.E., Patel, V.M., Chellappa, R.: Face-based active authentication on mobile devices. In: 2015 IEEE International Conference on Acoustics, Speech and Signal Processing (ICASSP), pp. 1687–1691 (2015)
24. Fenu, G., Marras, M., Boratto, L.: A multi-biometric system for continuous student authentication in e-learning platforms. Pattern Recogn. Lett. 113, 83–92 (2018). Integrating Biometrics and Forensics
25. Flior, E., Kowalski, K.: Continuous biometric user authentication in online examinations. In: 2010 Seventh International Conference on Information Technology: New Generations, pp. 488–492 (2010)
26. Frank, M., Biedert, R., Ma, E., Martinovic, I., Song, D.: Touchalytics: on the applicability of touchscreen input as a behavioral biometric for continuous authentication. IEEE Trans. Inf. Forensics Secur. 8(1), 136–148 (2013)
27. Furnell, S., Clarke, N.: Inhabiting the biometric society. ITNOW 60(3), 42–43 (2018)
28. Furnell, S., Clarke, N., Karatzouni, S.: Beyond the pin: enhancing user authentication for mobile devices. Computer Fraud & Security 2008(8), 12–17 (2008)
29. Garud, D., Agrwal, S.: Face liveness detection. In: 2016 International Conference on Automatic Control and Dynamic Optimization Techniques (ICACDOT), pp. 789–792 (2016)
30. Ghassemian, M., Smith-Creasey, M., Nekovee, M.: Secure non-public health enterprise networks. In: 2020 IEEE International Conference on Communications Workshops (ICC Workshops), pp. 1–6 (2020)
31. Gonzalez-Manzano, L., Fuentes, J.M.D., Ribagorda, A.: Leveraging user-related internet of things for continuous authentication: A survey. ACM Comput. Surv. 52(3), 1–38 (2019)
32. Gonzalez-Manzano, L., Mahbub, U., de Fuentes, J.M., Chellappa, R.: Impact of injection attacks on sensor-based continuous authentication for smartphones. Comput. Commun. 163, 150–161 (2020)
33. Géron, A.: Hands-on Machine Learning with Scikit-Learn and TensorFlow: Concepts, Tools, and Techniques to Build Intelligent Systems. O'Reilly Media, Sebastopol, CA (2017)
34. He, M., Horng, S.J., Fan, P., Run, R.S., Chen, R.J., Lai, J.L., Khan, M.K., Sentosa, K.O.: Performance evaluation of score level fusion in multimodal biometric systems. Pattern Recogn. 43(5), 1789–1800 (2010)

35. Horton, H.: 'phone zombies' see moped thefts on oxford street rocket 2100 per cent in two years, police data reveals. https://www.telegraph.co.uk/news/2018/02/15/phone-zombies-see-moped-thefts-oxford-street-rocket-2100-per/

36. Jain, A., Nandakumar, K., Ross, A.: Score normalization in multimodal biometric systems. Pattern Recogn. **38**(12), 2270–2285 (2005)

37. Jain, A.K., Deb, D., Engelsma, J.J.: Biometrics: Trust, but verify. CoRR **abs/2105.06625** (2021)

38. Jain, A.K., Ross, A., Prabhakar, S.: An introduction to biometric recognition. IEEE Trans. Circuits Syst. Video Technol. **14**(1), 4–20 (2004)

39. Jain, A.K., Ross, A.A., Nandakumar, K.: Introduction to Biometrics. Springer Publishing Company, Incorporated, Berlin (2011)

40. Kayacik, H.G., Just, M., Baillie, L., Aspinall, D., Micallef, N.: Data driven authentication: on the effectiveness of user behaviour modelling with mobile device sensors. arXiv preprint arXiv:1410.7743 (2014)

41. Khan, H., Hengartner, U., Vogel, D.: Usability and security perceptions of implicit authentication: convenient, secure, sometimes annoying. In: Eleventh Symposium On Usable Privacy and Security (SOUPS 2015), pp. 225–239. USENIX Association, Ottawa (2015)

42. Killourhy, K.S., Maxion, R.A.: Comparing anomaly-detection algorithms for keystroke dynamics. In: 2009 IEEE/IFIP International Conference on Dependable Systems & Networks, pp. 125–134 (2009)

43. Kumar, R., Kundu, P.P., Phoha, V.V.: Continuous authentication using one-class classifiers and their fusion. In: 2018 IEEE 4th International Conference on Identity, Security, and Behavior Analysis (ISBA), pp. 1–8 (2018)

44. Maguire, M.: The birth of biometric security. Anthropol. Today **25**(2), 9–14 (2009)

45. Mahfouz, A., Mahmoud, T.M., Eldin, A.S.: A survey on behavioral biometric authentication on smartphones. J. Inf. Secur. Appl. **37**, 28–37 (2017)

46. Mansfield, A.J., Wayman, J.L.: Best practices in testing and reporting performance of biometric devices. NPL report, Teddington (2002)

47. Matthew, P., Anderson, M.: Developing coercion detection solutions for biometrie security. In: 2016 SAI Computing Conference (SAI), pp. 1123–1130 (2016)

48. Micallef, N., Just, M., Baillie, L., Halvey, M., Kayacik, H.G.: Why aren't users using protection? investigating the usability of smartphone locking. In: Proceedings of the 17th International Conference on Human-Computer Interaction with Mobile Devices and Services, MobileHCI '15, pp. 284–294. Association for Computing Machinery, New York (2015)

49. Micallef, N., Kayacık, H.G., Just, M., Baillie, L., Aspinall, D.: Sensor use and usefulness: trade-offs for data-driven authentication on mobile devices. In: 2015 IEEE International Conference on Pervasive Computing and Communications (PerCom), pp. 189–197 (2015)

50. Mondal, S., Bours, P.: Continuous authentication using mouse dynamics. In: 2013 International Conference of the BIOSIG Special Interest Group (BIOSIG), pp. 1–12 (2013)

51. Mondal, S., Bours, P.: Swipe gesture based continuous authentication for mobile devices. In: 2015 International Conference on Biometrics (ICB), pp. 458–465 (2015)

52. Murphy, C., Huang, J., Hou, D., Schuckers, S.: Shared dataset on natural human-computer interaction to support continuous authentication research. In: 2017 IEEE International Joint Conference on Biometrics (IJCB), pp. 525–530 (2017)

53. Neal, T., Woodard, D.: Mobile biometrics, replay attacks, and behavior profiling: An empirical analysis of impostor detection. In: 2019 International Conference on Biometrics (ICB), pp. 1–8 (2019)

54. ONS: Mobile phone theft in the UK per annum. https://www.ons.gov.uk/aboutus/transparencyandgovernance/~freedomofinformationfoi/mobilephonetheftintheukperannum

55. Oza, P., Patel, V.M.: Federated learning-based active authentication on mobile devices. In: 2021 IEEE International Joint Conference on Biometrics (IJCB), pp. 1–8 (2021)

56. Phillips, P., Martin, A., Wilson, C., Przybocki, M.: An introduction to evaluating biometric systems. Computer **33**(2), 56–63 (2000)

57. Pourshahrokhi, N., Smith-Creasey, M., Ghassemian, M., Kouchaki, S.: Generative adversarial attacks on motion-based continuous authentication schemes. In: 2021 14th International Conference on Security of Information and Networks (SIN), vol. 1, pp. 1–6 (2021)
58. Rasnayaka, S., Saha, S., Sim, T.: Making the most of what you have! profiling biometric authentication on mobile devices. In: 2019 International Conference on Biometrics (ICB), pp. 1–7 (2019)
59. Rasnayaka, S., Sim, T.: Who wants continuous authentication on mobile devices? In: 2018 IEEE 9th International Conference on Biometrics Theory, Applications and Systems (BTAS), pp. 1–9 (2018)
60. Riva, O., Qin, C., Strauss, K., Lymberopoulos, D.: Progressive authentication: deciding when to authenticate on mobile phones. In: 21st USENIX Security Symposium, pp. 301–316. USENIX Association, Bellevue (2012)
61. Ross, A., Jain, A.: Information fusion in biometrics. Pattern Recogn. Lett. **24**(13), 2115–2125 (2003). Audio- and Video-based Biometric Person Authentication (AVBPA 2001)
62. Ross, A.A., Nandakumar, K., Jain, A.K.: Handbook of Multibiometrics, 1st edn. Springer Publishing Company, Incorporated, Berlin (2006)
63. Rossiter, D.G.: Past, present & future of information technology in pedometrics. Geoderma **324**, 131–137 (2018)
64. Ryu, R., Yeom, S., Kim, S.H., Herbert, D.: Continuous multimodal biometric authentication schemes: A systematic review. IEEE Access **9**, 34541–34557 (2021)
65. Samangouei, P., Patel, V.M., Chellappa, R.: Facial attributes for active authentication on mobile devices. Image Vis. Comput. **58**, 181–192 (2017)
66. Serwadda, A., Phoha, V.V.: Examining a large keystroke biometrics dataset for statistical-attack openings. ACM Trans. Inf. Syst. Secur. **16**(2), 1–30 (2013)
67. Serwadda, A., Phoha, V.V., Wang, Z., Kumar, R., Shukla, D.: Toward robotic robbery on the touch screen. ACM Trans. Inf. Syst. Secur. **18**(4), 1–25 (2016)
68. Shah, S.W., Kanhere, S.S.: Recent trends in user authentication—a survey. IEEE Access **7**, 112505–112519 (2019)
69. Shalf, J.: The future of computing beyond Moore's law. Phil. Trans. R. Soc. A **378**(2166), 20190061 (2020)
70. Shepard, C., Rahmati, A., Tossell, C., Zhong, L., Kortum, P.: LiveLab: measuring wireless networks and smartphone users in the field. SIGMETRICS Perform. Eval. Rev. **38**(3), 15–20 (2011)
71. Shepherd, S.J.: Continuous authentication by analysis of keyboard typing characteristics. In: European Convention on Security and Detection, 1995, pp. 111–114 (1995)
72. Sim, T., Zhang, S., Janakiraman, R., Kumar, S.: Continuous verification using multimodal biometrics. IEEE Trans. Pattern Anal. Mach. Intell. **29**(4), 687–700 (2007)
73. Sitová, Z., Šeděnka, J., Yang, Q., Peng, G., Zhou, G., Gasti, P., Balagani, K.S.: HMOG: New behavioral biometric features for continuous authentication of smartphone users. IEEE Trans. Inf. Forensics Secur. **11**(5), 877–892 (2016)
74. Sivasamy, M., Sastry, V., Gopalan, N.: VRCAuth: continuous authentication of users in virtual reality environment using head-movement. In: 2020 5th International Conference on Communication and Electronics Systems (ICCES), pp. 518–523 (2020)
75. Skalkos, A., Stylios, I., Karyda, M., Kokolakis, S.: Users privacy attitudes towards the use of behavioral biometrics continuous authentication (BBCA) technologies: A protection motivation theory approach. Journal of Cybersecurity and Privacy **1**(4), 743–766 (2021)
76. Smith-Creasey, M., Albalooshi, F.A., Rajarajan, M.: Context awareness for improved continuous face authentication on mobile devices. In: 2018 IEEE 16th International Conference on Dependable, Autonomic and Secure Computing, 16th International Conference on Pervasive Intelligence and Computing, 4th International Conference on Big Data Intelligence and Computing and Cyber Science and Technology Congress(DASC/PiCom/DataCom/CyberSciTech), pp. 644–652 (2018)

77. Smith-Creasey, M., Rajarajan, M.: A continuous user authentication scheme for mobile devices. In: 2016 14th Annual Conference on Privacy, Security and Trust (PST), pp. 104–113 (2016)
78. Smith-Creasey, M., Rajarajan, M.: Adaptive threshold scheme for touchscreen gesture continuous authentication using sensor trust. In: 2017 IEEE Trustcom/BigDataSE/ICESS, pp. 554–561 (2017)
79. Socolinsky, D., Selinger, A.: Thermal face recognition over time. In: Proceedings of the 17th International Conference on Pattern Recognition, 2004. ICPR 2004, vol. 4, pp. 187–190 (2004)
80. Stylios, I.C., Thanou, O., Androulidakis, I., Zaitseva, E.: A review of continuous authentication using behavioral biometrics. In: Proceedings of the SouthEast European Design Automation, Computer Engineering, Computer Networks and Social Media Conference, SEEDA-CECNSM '16, pp. 72–79. Association for Computing Machinery, New York (2016)
81. Surowiecki, J.: The Wisdom of Crowds. Anchor (2005)
82. Uludag, U., Jain, A.K.: Attacks on biometric systems: a case study in fingerprints. In: Security, steganography, and watermarking of multimedia contents VI, vol. 5306, pp. 622–633. SPIE, New York (2004)
83. Vural, E., Huang, J., Hou, D., Schuckers, S.: Shared research dataset to support development of keystroke authentication. In: IEEE International Joint Conference on Biometrics, pp. 1–8 (2014)
84. Wayman, J.L., Jain, A.K., Maltoni, D., Maio, D.: Biometric systems: technology, design and performance evaluation. Springer Science & Business Media, Berlin (2005)
85. Weiss, G.M., Yoneda, K., Hayajneh, T.: Smartphone and smartwatch-based biometrics using activities of daily living. IEEE Access **7**, 133190–133202 (2019)
86. Wen, C.: Chapter 8—telemedicine, ehealth and remote care systems. In: de Fátima Marin, H., Massad, E., Gutierrez, M.A., Rodrigues, R.J., Sigulem, D. (eds.) Global Health Informatics, pp. 168–194. Academic Press, New York (2017)
87. Xu, H., Zhou, Y., Lyu, M.R.: Towards continuous and passive authentication via touch biometrics: an experimental study on smartphones. In: 10th Symposium On Usable Privacy and Security (SOUPS 2014), pp. 187–198. USENIX Association, Menlo Park (2014)
88. Yao, F., Yerima, S.Y., Kang, B., Sezer, S.: Event-driven implicit authentication for mobile access control. In: 2015 9th International Conference on Next Generation Mobile Applications, Services and Technologies, pp. 248–255 (2015)

Chapter 4
Biometrics for Continuous Authentication

4.1 Introduction

There are many biometrics that yield authentication accuracies acceptable for real-world use. Continuous biometric authentication systems, by definition, require the continuous (or at least frequent) collection of biometrics. However, not all biometrics are suitable of being collected continuously and transparently; many require an overt prompt to obtain a user's attention and request biometric input by the user. For example, the use of fingerprints may not be suitable for a continuous biometric authentication system because they cannot feasibly be collected continuously and transparently as the normal usage is conducted on a device [21]. In the last decade the utilisation of sensors on user devices has led to the continuous and transparent collection of biometrics for authentication. Some of these biometrics (such as touchscreen gestures [44]) have been proposed only recently. This increase in available biometrics is due to the enhanced sensing capabilities on devices today.

As discussed, the use of traditional biometrics within continuous authentication systems requires consideration due to the continuous nature of the collection process. Some factors must be taken into consideration that are not present when collecting biometrics for *one-shot* biometric authentication. This is because the biometrics are collected transparently, and therefore a greater amount of noise may be present (e.g., illumination from the environment in continuous face collection [115]). As such, the collection of these biometrics may result in a need for greater pre-processing to remove noise and may also produce lower authentication accuracies.

M. Smith-Creasey, *Continuous Biometric Authentication Systems*, SpringerBriefs in Computer Science, https://doi.org/10.1007/978-3-031-49071-2_4

4.2 Requirements

Selecting the most suitable biometric is a process that requires careful consideration. The most accurate biometric may not always be the most suitable biometric to employ within a system; users may feel uncomfortable providing the biometric or it may be a biometric that not everybody has. When reviewing the available biometric modalities, it is important to assess them against a well-known set of requirements [62] (originally proposed in 2004) which allows designers to select the most appropriate modalities for the system. The primary requirements are summarised as follows (and will be discussed within the context of usage in a continuous authentication scheme):

- **Universality**: This specifies that the trait should be held by everyone that may access the system. A system relying on traits of only men or only women would be limiting and hold low universality. However, even with popular traits, some conditions may make it difficult to achieve absolute universality, e.g., a rare genetic disorder called *adermatoglyphia* prevents fingerprint development [29].
- **Distinctiveness**: The distinctiveness (or uniqueness) requirement relies on the chosen biometric trait being sufficiently different for different people. Biometric traits that show high distinctiveness will have low FAR and FRR rates [64].
- **Permanence**: This requires a trait to have significant temporal permanence. This means that a trait should not be highly susceptible to rapid change. If a biometric trait were to change regularly, it would cause a high FRR [64].
- **Collectability**: The collectability of a trait refers to the ease of collecting and measuring the trait quantitatively. A trait such as deoxyribonucleic acid (DNA) is highly distinctive and permanent but is not easily collectable and requires specialist equipment to measure.

It should be noted that there is no model to quantify the uniqueness and permanence of biometric modalities[1] (even the knowledge on the uniqueness and permanence of the four most studied traits (fingerprint, face, iris, and voice) is incomplete) [95]. Some further criteria that are usually also considered in the literature due to their practical benefits in biometric systems are the following [62]:

- **Performance**: This refers to the performance as measured by metrics such as the error rates (e.g., EER, FAR, and FRR) and the computational time and resource requirements. Optimal systems should yield low error rates with low computational requirements, but sometimes there is a trade-off between these.
- **Acceptability**: The acceptability of a system refers to the acceptance of the system and the biometric traits by individuals in the target population [64]. Many smartphone users have little issue with authenticating their face, but some other more personal, private, or intrusive traits (e.g., DNA) may not be acceptable.

---

[1] However, some estimates have been made. Francis Galton estimated that two fingerprints from two people had a chance of 1 in 64 billion of matching [118], but the true figures are not known.

- **Circumvention**: This refers to how robust the biometric trait is against physical imitation by artifacts (in the case of physiological biometrics) or mimicry (in the case of behavioural biometrics) [64].

It is important to note that few biometric modalities will score consistently highly for each requirement. Furthermore, sometimes two requirements may be incompatible for a given modality. An example of this would be DNA, which scores highly on distinctiveness but low on acceptability. The selection of the optimal biometric modality will depend on the requirements that are most important for the system. Several further requirements that can be considered for *continuous* biometric systems include:

- **Continuousness**: The continuousness requirement refers to the extent that the biometric modality can be collected continuously. This differs for different biometrics. For example, the continuousness of a face is likely greater than that of a fingerprint since it is likely more available during device usage.
- **Transparency**: The aspect of transparency refers to the extent that the collection of the biometric is transparent to the user. This has been suggested in [26] to evaluate biometrics. Those biometric modalities that explicitly request interaction with a sensor would score low on transparency, whereas those that are transparently and implicitly collected during device usage would score higher.

There are a variety of requirements defined in the literature that optimal biometric modalities should satisfy. However, no modality can score highly on every requirement. Nonetheless it is important to decide on which requirements are important for the system and consider how the potential biometric modalities score against these requirements.

4.3 Functionality

The collection, processing, and matching of biometrics can facilitate two different identity management functionalities. These are known as *identification* and *verification* [64]. These two functionalities rely on similar techniques but are vastly different in purpose. The following describes how these two functionalities utilise biometrics:

- **Verification**: The process of performing verification attempts to match a biometric data of a claimed identity to the biometric profile of that claimed identity. Verification is therefore a check to see if the user is the identity they claim [64]. This process is a one-to-one comparison. The resulting match similarity will subsequently result in the user either being verified and identified as the identity they claim or being rejected and identified as an impostor (whose identity is unknown). Prior to providing a system their biometrics, a user may claim an identity via providing a username, presenting a smartcard, or (as is the case for modern devices) accessing a non-public device. The process of verification carries multiple advantages over identification. Firstly, a verification system can be trained relatively quickly because it needs only train the system on biometric data for a single identity (i.e., no large database is needed). Secondly, because the comparison is a one-to-one process, a match can be provided faster and with less processing than systems where multiple identity checks are required. It must be noted that *authentication* is often used as a synonym for verification [64].

- **Identification**: Systems performing identification attempt to match biometric data collected from a user to a database containing many biometric profiles. This enables the system to find if a user (based on their biometrics) is known to the system or not. This requires a comparison with all stored biometric profiles in the database (which can cause performance overhead for large databases). This process is therefore considered a one-to-many problem. The profile in the database with the highest similarity to the probe biometric data is considered the matched identity (known as *closed set identification*), though a threshold may also be enforced to consider the profile a match (known as *open set identification*) [64]. The process of identification is often divided into two further purposes known as *positive* and *negative* recognition [64]. In positive recognition the purpose is find if some biometric data without an explicit identity matches a profile known to the system (useful for checking fingerprints in criminal databases). The purpose of negative recognition is to ensure biometric data from a user is not already enrolled in the database so as to prevent multiple profiles for the same user (useful in preventing multiple sign-ups to government services). However, one must be careful with identification systems because as the database size grows the probability of a false match can grow significantly. In a system where matching two profiles gives a probability of 0.1% false acceptance, for a database of 7,000 people a user would have a 99.91% probability of being falsely accepted [33]. This is formulated as $P_N = 1 - (1 - P_1)^N$, where P_1 is the probability of false acceptance in verification, P_N the probability of a false acceptance in identification, and N the size of the database.

4.4   Modalities

The term *biometric modality* refers to a specific biometric, such as a face or a fingerprint. The term is often synonymous with *biometric characteristics*, *traits*, *indicators*, and *identifiers* [64]. There are many different biometric modalities that exist. Some modalities have been used for centuries, whereas others have been proposed more recently. The modalities are often categorised as either *physiological* or *behavioural* [96]. There have been a variety of biometric modalities proposed for use in the continuous biometric authentication domain. Some of these have gathered more popularity than others, with one review indicating that in multi-modal approaches the keystroke dynamics modality was the most used modality [96]. As in Leonardo da Vinci's *Vitruvian Man* (showing that human anatomy follows some proportionality), some recent studies have shown that there is an amount of inference possible between some modalities (known as *cross-modal* biometric matching [86]).

4.4.1 Physiological

Biometric modalities that are considered physiological are those that are a direct result of an individual's unique physical traits [96]. For example, the face and the fingerprint are a physiological biometric modalities because they are both physiological characteristics of an individual. The *Bertillon System*, developed in the 1800s by French police officer Alphonse Bertillon, for criminal identification was a system built upon the idea of recognising individuals by their unique physiological modalities [16]. This section focuses on some physiological modalities that have been explored within the context of continuous biometric authentication systems.

4.4.1.1 Face

Human faces vary significantly from person to person and there is recent evidence to suggest that human faces have evolved to signal individual identity (especially when contrasted with other traits of the body and the uniform appearances of other animals) [106]. Recognising each other by our faces is something that humans are innately capable of doing. Our brains are believed to be hardwired to recognise faces through the *fusiform face area*, a part of the brain that responds strongly to faces [67]. This is perhaps why faces are one of the primary ways we, as a society, recognise each other [64]. However, whilst we take the concept of recognising faces for granted, it has been a significant and ongoing research challenge to get computer systems to replicate this behaviour. Even humans differ in the way we recognise faces (with Malaysian Chinese looking at faces differently to recognise them than both Westerners and Mainland Chinese [120]). Though, in recent years, computational approaches to face recognition now surpass human abilities [74].

The process of face recognition comprises three steps: (i) image capture, (ii) face detection, and (iii) face matching [64]. The first of these steps requires a sensor that can capture the face. In most user devices (e.g., smartphones and laptops) this is most commonly a camera capable of capturing 2D images (though 3D images can be captured from devices with infrared capabilities, like the *Apple iPhone*). Images captured from device cameras are represented by a two-dimensional pixel array in which the red, green, and blue channels are each represented by 8 bits, providing $2^8 = 256$ variations per channel and $2^{24} = 16,777,216$ colour variations in total. However, it is common for studies to reduce the size of the image and convert coloured images to grey scale because this reduces the processing required.

The second step in the face recognition process is searching for the captured image to detect any faces contained within it. The *Viola–Jones* algorithm (named after its creators) computes an integral image over the input image to detect shading that may indicate a face to enable fast evaluation via boosted weak classifiers based on Haar-like features [124]. The approach is popular because it can be applied accurately in real time but can suffer from illumination, occlusion, and pose angle. The application of deep learning techniques to computer vision problems in the last decade has seen success in producing solutions to face detection in unconstrained scenarios such as the multi-task convolutional neural network approach in [131]. Many face detection algorithms are freely available in libraries such as *OpenCV*[2] and *dlib*.[3]

The final step is to match the probe face (or its features) against that of a template of the expected face. Sometimes there is a pre-processing stage before the matching that aligns the face or performs histogram equalisation to reduce illumination variations [40]. The pre-processed face can then be matched via a template or a machine learning model. Researchers have spent decades trying to produce accurate and robust face recognition techniques. Early solutions proposed included solutions such as Eigenfaces, but these were often sensitive to face variation. Some works have shown that textual features represented by histograms of oriented gradients (HOG) or local binary patterns (LBP) can be used to train classifiers to deliver competitive face recognition results [116]. The advent of deep learning approaches has progressed the field significantly with approaches obtaining accuracies of 99.87% [65].

The cameras contained in many modern user devices (including smartphones, tablets, and laptops) are well suited to capturing the face for continuous authentication because the face of the user is likely to be available during usage. This has encouraged the use of facial biometrics in continuous authentication studies [90]. It is important to note the nuances of the faces collected by different devices to understand the challenges that a continuous face authentication system may need to overcome. In [26] the author notes that desktop computers may expect fairly consistent frontal faces, but smartphones may contain greater noise, movement, occlusion, and environmental variation (e.g., illumination). The author further discusses that the angle a face image is captured increases the false rejection rate as it moves further from the norm.

There are difficulties in applying traditional face recognition techniques to continuous authentication systems. Some of the captured continuous face datasets show the extreme variation in pose during the use of a mobile device caused by the movement of the head or of the device (possibly due to user activity such as walking [116]). A face, being a social organ, is also variable due to the face movements performed to exhibit social ques [34]. This presents images that may be highly variable, partially occluded, or of poor quality. In [77] the authors present a scheme based on deep neural networks to detect partial faces that techniques such as Viola–Jones fail to detect. This can enable face recognition to be conducted on the available face attributes. The intra-class variations of collected faces can be significant in different conditions.

---

[2] https://opencv.org/.

[3] http://dlib.net/.

Continuous face-based authentication techniques have been considered since 2001 where it was suggested to use a computer webcam to continuously collect faces [70]. Another early study, from 2008, explored continuous facial authentication on mobile devices was [28]. They compare common face recognition algorithms (e.g., Eigenfaces) on the FERET dataset containing faces collected at different angles. They show a composite facial template made of faces collected from different angles yielded lower FRRs than that of a single orientation. In [31] the authors also attempt to solve the angular differences that are present in collected faces. They do this via utilising accelerometer, gyroscope, and magnetometer data to orient the face image to a pose from which facial regions can be extracted and classified. Utilising commercial face-matching software (*PittPatt*), they show that 96% of genuine users were never falsely rejected and 89% of impostors detected within 2 minutes. The scheme achieves good accuracy but only authenticates once every 30 seconds.

In a 2015 study on continuous face-based authentication on smartphones, the authors analyse a variety of different facial recognition algorithms (e.g., Eigenfaces and Fisherfaces) on their dataset containing videos of faces in different illumination conditions [40]. They extracted the eyes, nose, and mouth for recognition. Their results indicate that illumination can have a deleterious impact on the recognition accuracy when a system is trained on faces from a different illumination to that which it is tested on. The authors in [101] use a different approach and utilise 44 facial attributes (including 'moustache', 'male', and 'round jaw'). Their system works by extracting HOG and LBP features from facial regions with and without certain attributes for training a set of SVM classifiers. Users are enrolled by their score of each attribute that forms an attribute profile that the attributes of future face samples can be compared to. Using a dataset containing various illumination conditions, they report an EER of 30% for mixed sessions and 13–14% for illumination matched sessions. However, no effort is made to create approaches for minimising the impact of illumination variation. The authors expand on this work in [102] where they implement the system on actual smartphones. They decrease the EERs via parameter tuning and authenticate at a rate of 4 frames per second (FPS).

Many studies have focused explicitly on authentication, without considering other necessities of continuous biometric authentication systems such as context awareness and liveness detection. In [116] the authors look at not only illumination but also the impact of activities (sitting, standing, and walking) on face authentication. There was a significant degradation in EER when faces from a walking activity and were mixed with the other two activities. The study also proposed extracting HOG and LBP features from facial attributes for classification in an SVM for liveness detection. Some recent face-based neural networks (such as VGG and FaceNet) were shown as vulnerable to deep fakes (faces generated via generative neural networks (GANs)) [71], though these might be detected if presented to the camera sensor in a system employing liveness detection. In [115] the authors utilised accelerometer data in LSTM networks to classify activity and data from the light sensor in a logistic regression classifier to detect illumination. Utilising the detected contexts, the authors built a *context-aware* continuous face-based authentication system that selected facial templates for comparison that were suited to the detected context. This approach showed an improvement in EERs in both contexts.

4.4.1.2   Iris

Eyes have several unique physiological characteristics that have been proven to be suitable for authentication, including the retina and the iris. However, the most extensively investigated eye biometric is the iris [64]. The iris is the annular structure between the white of the eye (the sclera) and the pupil and controls the diameter of the pupil (thus controlling the amount of light entering through the pupil and reaching the retina). In 1949, British ophthalmologist J. H. Doggart observed that the "minute architecture of the iris exhibit variations in every subject examined." These variations are features such as furrows, ridges, and crypts [34]. In 1994, John Daugman was granted a patent detailing an algorithm for iris recognition which has formed the foundations for many subsequent iris recognition systems (including many still in use). Today, iris recognition is a common and robust method of biometric authentication because it provides a unique and stable biometric that can be quickly and accurately evaluated [26]. The iris has such distinguishing properties that iris recognition has even been shown to be possible 21 days after death [123].

The process of performing iris recognition begins with image acquisition, a process that generally uses a camera sensitive to near-infrared (NIR) light and a source of NIR light to illuminate the iris [64]. The use of NIR light is due to the difficulty resolving the intricate textures of the iris (especially for darker eye colours, such as brown eyes) in RGB channels. Iris segmentation (a field within its own right) then occurs to localise and segment the iris from the pupil and sclera. Once the iris has been located and segmented, a geometric normalisation (via Daugman's rubber sheet model [64]) can be applied to 'unwrap' the iris and represent it as a rectangle. The normalised iris is processed using 2D Gabor wavelets, producing a sequence of phasors that are quantised to form a string of bits [34]. This string of bits is known as an *IrisCode* and is commonly 2048 bits in length. The Hamming distance is the metric used to compute similarity between two iris codes, and those from the same eye are expected to be smaller than that of two different eyes. A collection of resources for iris recognition is available from John Daugman on his website.[4]

The iris is an optimal biometric in many ways, though it has been sparsely applied within the realm of continuous authentication. Whilst it is a biometric that would be expected to be continuously and transparently obtainable as a user fixates their gaze on a device to operate it, the iris requires near-infrared. A continuous iris recognition scheme is produced in [82] using a commercial eye tracker device and yields an EER of 11% when tested on 37 users. However, the approach is dependent on an external device and not explored within the context of user devices. In [88], researchers with Samsung produce an iris feature extracting and matching mechanism based on

---

[4] https://www.cl.cam.ac.uk/~jgd1000/.

lightweight convolutional neural networks for mobile devices. The scheme yields an EER of 10%. However, few continuous authentication schemes employ irises due to optimal results needing near-infrared cameras (which not all devices have) and also due to common occlusion issues [64]. Several factors make continuous iris recognition difficult. The first is the lack of NIR functionality in user devices (iris recognition was implemented in the *Samsung Galaxy S8*, but the functionality was discontinued in later devices). The second factor is due to the potential for noise in continuously collected irises; accurate recognition requires at least 50% of the iris and capturing eyelashes, hair, or partial blinks can hinder recognition [34].

4.4.1.3 Photoplethysmography

The human heart is a fascinating organ that circulates blood throughout the body. It does this by contracting as a result of an electrical impulse generated by a group of pacemaker cells in the sinoatrial node. This behaviour is a heartbeat. The frequency of heartbeats is the heart rate (HR), which is often measured in beats per minute (BPM). The heart rate is a highly variable physiological biometric, and it can be affected by exercise, stress, temperature, and various ions (sodium, calcium, and potassium) in the blood [17]. Wearable technologies such as smartwatches and fitness bands have grown in popularity recently and many use photoplethysmography (PPG) to measure heart rate [128]. This is done with a light emitting diode (LED) and a photo-diode (PD) which are often placed in contact with a user's skin. The reflected light obtained by the PD is different when the blood volume is low compared to when the blood volume is high, enabling blood volume (and therefore heartbeats) to be captured.

The PPG sensors in wearables has motivated research into using the readings (representative of the hemodynamics and cardiovascular system [128]) as a phys-iological biometric. When obtained from a sensor that remains on a user's person during daily activities, the signal may contain *motion artefacts*; these are incorrect readings (e.g., false peaks) arising due to user movement [134]. Such motion artefacts can degrade the accuracy and are often identified and removed before the signal is authenticated. There are two approaches commonly explored for PPG-based authentication, and these are either focused on the *fiducial* points of the signal (such as the systolic and diastolic peaks) or focused on *non-fiducial* signal-based features.

In 2013, a preliminary study showed that photoplethysmography had potential to continuously authenticate users [20]. Other studies have verified this, such as [128] in which the authors produce a non-fiducial authentication approach for fingertip-based PPG signals. They first pre-process the signals (e.g., by removing motion artefacts and segmenting the signal) and subsequently extract features using a Continuous Wavelet Transform (CWT) and reduce dimensionality using Direct Linear Discriminant Analysis (DLDA). Finally, classification is done by computing Pearson's distance between training templates and test vectors. They achieved EERs of 0.5–6% on data from different conditions (e.g., physical stress). The authors in [134] show a wrist-based continuous authentication system based on PPG. The approach first filters the signal to reduce noise and remove or mitigate different types of motion artefacts. Some general fiducial features are extracted and classified with a Gradient Boosting Tree (GBT) to authenticate the user. They achieve an accuracy of 90.73% when testing on PPG signals obtained from the wrists of 20 users.

There are a variety of benefits in utilising PPG signals to continuously authenticate users via wearables. Firstly, it is the case that a continuous PPG stream is already available on many wearables (such as some *Fitbit* devices) and consumes little power (e.g., 4 mA [133]) relative to the battery capacity. Furthermore, unlike some other biometrics based on the cardiovascular system, such as an ECG (see Sect. 4.4.1.5), PPG implemented in wearables only requires one point of contact with the skin. Such a biometric would also be difficult to spoof without knowledge of a user's cardiovascular activity. However, there is a considerable variability in PPG, and it can also be susceptible to interference from motion artefacts. There is also evidence of concept drift when data is authenticated after a two-week gap [128].

4.4.1.4 Ear

In *Hannibal*, the 1999 bestseller by Thomas Harris, an Italian detective named Rinaldo Pazzi compares images of the serial killer Hannibal Lecter to the curator of the Capponi Library. Pazzi does not find a sufficient match in the face, but learning from the methods of Alphonse Bertillon 100 years before him uses the ears to find a promising match. Bertillon, in his 1890 seminal work on biometrics, described the ear as the "most significant factor from the point of view of identification" because of the "multiple small valleys and hills which furrow across it" [15]. The ear has several advantages as a biometric modality [60]. Firstly, the ear has a rich and stable structure that does not change a significant amount over time. Secondly, the ear is not subject to change based on emotion, as is the case with the face. The visible part of the ear is known as the *pinna*, the morphology of which is considered to be unique to an individual [64]. The pinna has an intricate structure comprised of various anatomical components such as the helix rim, lobule, concha, tragus, and antitragus. The process of authentication for an ear follows one similar to that of the face, since it is a modality often captured via a camera. In this process an ear is first detected to allow discriminative features (e.g., represented via LBPs) to be extracted and then classified to produce a final decision on the authenticity [64].

There have been several authentication systems proposed using ears detected from device cameras as a way to authenticate users. These studies often create systems for smartphones for the purpose of authentication during a call. In [8], the system is designed to authenticate the user as the smartphone is lifted to the ear to take a call. Similarly, in [1], the authors detect the ear (via the Viola–Jones algorithm) as smartphones are raised to the ear to receive a call. They use LBP features extracted from the ear with Euclidean distance measures between biometric feature vectors to produce a score. In the study the ear produced an EER of 17.7%. One other way the ear shows potential as a modality for authenticating is using the ear canal. In [50], the authors show how reflections of sounds emitted down the unique ear canal can continuously authenticate users. Their approach achieved a precision of 97.57%. The obvious downside of using the ear for continuous authentication is that the device must often be next to or against an ear which, in many situations, is not feasible.

4.4.1.5 Electrocardiogram

In 1842, an Italian professor of physics at the University of Pisa, Dr Carlo Matteucci, showed that electrical current accompanied every heartbeat in frogs [7]. This discovery led to numerous developments over the subsequent decades, not least by Dr Willem Einthoven who was in 1924 awarded the Nobel Prize in physiology and medicine for his contributions to electrocardiography [7]. The electrocardiogram (ECG) is a plot of the voltage versus time as measured from the electrical activity of the heart via electrodes placed on the skin. The reading between a pair of electrodes is known as a *lead*. Traditionally, ECGs have been performed *on-the-person* with 10 electrodes placed directly on the skin for a 12-lead ECG in clinical environments for in-depth medical diagnostics [61]. The other form of ECG is *off-the-person* which utilises no special preparation and can obtain a convenient 1-lead ECG via wearables or portable devices with pairs of dry electrodes [61]. The resulting ECG waveform contains five deflections (waves), denoted as P, Q, R, S, and T, with each representing an electrical event in the heart. The resulting ECG reading differs due to gender, heart mass orientation, conductivity, and activation order of cardiac muscles [13]. These differences cause traits that allow for the identification of individuals [19].

Numerous studies have proposed approaches for utilising ECG signals for authentication. Most ECG-based authentication schemes follow a series of steps including signal sensing, filtering (e.g., via the Kalman Filter), segmentation (into an ECG for a single heartbeat), feature extraction, and matching [61]. The authors in [32] construct a system that places two electrodes into a keyboard wrist rest and collects 2 minutes of ECG data. The EERs for experiments when trained and tested on data from the same session were as low as 1–2%, but this increased to 9% when there was a 4-month interval between sessions. In [103], a relatively low-cost consumer-grade ECG monitor (from *AliveCor*) is used to collect signals from which SVMs are trained. The study reported an EER of 2.44% when training and testing data were from the same session, but the EER rose to 9.65% when tested on data 4 months from the training data (validating the increase in EER seen in [32]). Utilising a stream of ECG data for continuous authentication is proposed in [24]. An ECG data stream captured from 10 users is used to produce a system with accuracies of up to 96% that can dynamically adapt to minor changes (e.g., due to stress).

ECG has the benefit of being a biometric that is difficult (but not impossible [35]) to forge as it is not visible to attackers (unlike the face) and does not leave a trace whilst authenticating (unlike with fingerprints) [13]. However, one of the key limitations of ECG authentication is the need for specialised hardware not

commonly included on modern devices (other than some wearable devices) [13].
Furthermore, ECG biometrics may not be well suited to continuous authentication
because a user would likely be required to maintain a connection with a pair of
electrodes, which may be inconvenient and impractical. There are also questions of
permanence in ECG data because studies with intervals between training and testing
data consistently show increases in EERs, even if the interval is only a matter of days
[91].

4.4.2 Behavioural

In *The Sign of Four*, the second novel of the *Sherlock Holmes* series, Holmes
explains to Dr Watson that a statistician may predict the behaviour of a group but
'never foretell what any one man will do'. Since this was written in 1890, the
researchers in the field of *behavioural* biometrics have built behavioural profiles
containing models capable of accurately foretelling whether what a user does
(i.e., their behaviour) is expected. These profiles utilise the unique behaviours and
habits of individuals, such as their gait or keystroke dynamics. Many continuous
biometric authentication systems now make use of such behavioural profiles, with
most of the studies in the literature utilising behavioural modalities [6]. This
may be because such modalities are considered more universal and transparent
than physiological modalities [26]. This section describes some of the behavioural
modalities researched.

Behavioural modalities can have greater variance between samples than physiological modalities because behaviour is prone to greater fluctuation than physiology.
Some of this variance may be explained with psychology because performance tends
to improve over time, with more significant improvements seen at the beginning
(known as the *power law of practice*) [53]. Therefore, situations in which data
are collected from a user performing a behavioural task they have not previously
done (e.g., typing on a smartphone keyboard) may not be optimal to compare later
samples to when the user has had significant practice. This is not often considered
within continuous behavioural biometric systems but may benefit performance if
users were provided time to get accustomed to tasks they are new to [38].

4.4.2.1 Keystroke Dynamics

During World War II, some of the communications were sent using Morse code
via a telegraph. It has been reported that subtle time differences and rhythm of
the dots and dashes forming the letters were enough for some telegraph operators
to identify the sender of a message. This distinctive operator pattern was known
as the *fist of the sender* [66] and carries many similarities to the modern field of
keystroke dynamics, which looks for nuances in the user's typing patterns. These
typing patterns are often based on the differences in timings during and between key

presses. Using keyboard interactions as a way to authenticate users was suggested as early as 1975 where the *way* a password was typed (such as key press timings) would also be used to authenticate [117]. In 1995, a study proposed a system for an IBM PC that performed 'continuous analysis of the typing characteristics of the user for the purpose of continuous authentication' [109]. Keystroke dynamics has grown significantly as a field since the early 2000s [121] and has been investigated to continuously authenticate users on a variety of devices.

Studies authenticating keystroke dynamics are split into two key categories. The first is known as *text-dependent* (or *static*) and requires a specific word or phrase in order to authenticate [26]. The second is known as *text-independent* (or *dynamic*) and can authenticate whilst any text is typed [26]. The latter is better for continuous authentication systems because it can be deployed transparently [30]. However, text-independent systems can require considerable training data (as they must work for all textual input) which can take days to collect. Also, these systems may yield lower accuracies than text-dependent systems [84], as they may not have seen the input before. The features extracted from keystroke dynamics used for authentication are often based on keystroke timings. These timings are usually taken from monographs (hold time of a key press) and digraphs (timings between two key presses) [14]. The different monographs and digraphs that can be extracted can be seen in Fig. 4.1. Involving more keys for trigraphs and *n*-graphs has also been considered, but these often do not appear frequently enough in training sets [14]. On devices capable of detecting pressure and movement, these features can also be utilised [112].

One of the first experiments on authenticating via keystroke dynamics was conducted in 1997 and achieved accuracies of 90.7 and 23.0% for text-dependent and text-independent approaches, respectively [84]. An algorithm was proposed in a 2005 study [51] for comparing freely typed text, based on 'R' (relative) and 'A' (absolute) features of *n*-graphs. They achieve a FAR of 0.005% and a FRR of 5% and still achieve competitive accuracies in modern studies [59]. In 2009 a continuous authentication scheme is proposed using at least 6 days of typing data from 25

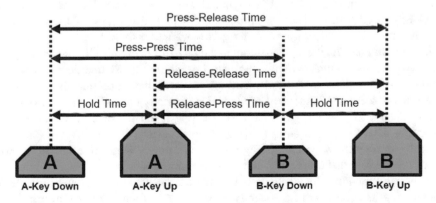

Fig. 4.1 Showing the monograph and digraph features obtained for key presses of the 'A' and 'B' keys

users, and through statistical comparisons (via mean and standard deviation) of monographs and digraphs, impostors were detected after 79–348 keystrokes [21]. In [85], a dataset was released capturing the typing behaviour from 103 users in completely uncontrolled conditions over a period of 2.5 years. This was used in [59] where the authors introduced a keystroke dynamics algorithm based on kernel density estimation (KDE). They benchmark their technique with other algorithms by training the system on 10,000 keystrokes and testing it on 1,000 keystrokes. Their technique achieves the lowest EER of 7.59%, with that in [51] achieving the next lowest EER of 10.36%. It has been shown that approaches used for keystroke dynamics still perform adequately over time and between different languages for users [52].

Of course, keyboards are an interface not only to traditional computer systems but also to smartphones and tablets. The feasibility of using keystroke dynamics on phones was explored in 2007 in [27] where the authors explored the feasibility of authenticating telephone numbers and typing text messages. Using neural network classifiers, they were able to achieve average an EER of 12.8%. There have since been recommendations to utilise the trend of smartphones incorporating touchscreens to devise new features for typing [30]. Given that smartphones have additional sensors such as an accelerometer and gyroscope, it has also been shown that these can be used to compute the unique grasp and resistance movement qualities for individuals to continuously authenticate typing behaviour with EERs as low as 7.16% [112]. However, keystroke dynamics for continuous authentication is naturally limited to the times in which the user is typing. Furthermore, using keystroke dynamics may come with privacy considerations because such behaviour can also be utilised as a soft biometric to infer the gender of the user [22].

4.4.2.2 Mouse Dynamics

When computers first gained popularity, they did not use a computer mouse and were instead controlled with only a keyboard. During the 1960s, Douglas Englebart and Bill English developed the initial concept and technology of the computer mouse. In 1967, a patent for an *X–Y Position Indicator for a Display System* was filed by Douglas Englebart and granted in 1970 [39]. Today this technology is known better as a computer *mouse* because of the similarity of a traditional computer mouse (with a wire) to the rodent. Much research has gone into the computer mouse, not least within the field of HCI. For example, the well-known *Fitts Law*, now integral to GUI design, relates to the time taken to perform a task with a pointing device (e.g., a mouse) [92]. Of course, users will naturally use a mouse slightly differently when controlling a computer cursor (e.g., in terms of speed). This unique way that users move and operate a mouse has been shown as a feasible behavioural modality for continuous biometric authentication systems [92]. As a device that is common and frequently used during a computer session, using the mouse for authentication has the benefit of not being intrusive and requiring no special hardware [83].

In [83], the authors present a continuous authentication system utilising mouse dynamics. The authors utilise a publicly available dataset of mouse movements from 49 volunteers as they use their mouse and computer in a normal and unrestricted way. The dataset stored the type of event (e.g., movement or point and click), travelled distance, elapsed time, and the direction of movement. The classification was done by building an SVM for each user. Using a personalised threshold for each user, the authors found genuine users were never classified as impostors in a session and the average number of mouse actions an impostor could perform before detection was 94. In another mouse dynamics-based continuous authentication system, the authors use mouse movements, point and click, and drag and drop behaviours [9]. The highest accuracies achieved for authentication using Decision Trees, K-Nearest Neighbours, and Random Forest classifiers were 87.6%, 99.3%, and 89.9%, respectively.

The use of mouse dynamics as a behavioural biometric in continuous authentication systems has been shown to yield impressive accuracies in some studies. This is also a modality that sees wide usage, with minimal computation, low intrusiveness, and (in most cases) no additional equipment required. However, it should be noted that many users will utilise a variety of different mice throughout the day. These different mice may have differing settings and hardware. When this is the case (as for any technology), it cannot be assumed that a model built for a user for one mouse will translate well to a user's use of another mouse.

4.4.2.3 Touchscreen Gestures

Touchscreens have been employed on user devices (such as mobile phones) since the 2000s, but these early screens were implemented using resistive touchscreens which restricted the fluidity and nuances of user input (often requiring a stylus). In 2007, the first mobile phones were released with capacitive touchscreens, including the *LG Prada* and the *Apple iPhone*. When Steve Jobs, then Apple CEO, announced the iPhone launch at an Apple keynote address, he made the argument that a stylus was an inconvenient and antiquated form of interacting with a touchscreen when we already have 10 natural styluses on our hands. Today capacitive touchscreens are the predominant method to implement a mobile touchscreen [18] and are in use in a multitude of other user devices including laptops, smartwatches, and tablet computers, to improve human–computer interaction (HCI) for the user.

The touchscreen interactions that users perform to interact with a device are often known in the literature as touchscreen *gestures* [43]. In order to respond to a touchscreen gesture (such as a swipe to scroll through a web page), a device will obtain and process information about the gesture in real time. The information collected from a touchscreen gesture is comprised of multiple *touch events* [44]. A touch event commonly includes a timestamp, the x and y coordinates of the finger, the area of the finger, and the pressure applied to the screen. The full gesture can therefore be represented as a collection of touch event vectors. The time between touch events may vary because they are created as the finger moves to new pixel locations and therefore may vary based on the speed of the finger, and a median frequency of 17 ms was reported in [44]. This data can be obtained from some APIs, such as that of the *Android* mobile operating system via the *MotionEvent*[5] class.

There have been numerous recent studies on the information that touchscreen gestures reveal about a user. In [11], it was found that touchscreen gestures could be used as a soft biometric to reveal group identity such as the gender and the level of touchscreen experience. In [18], a similar study was performed on 19,000 gestures belonging to 178 users where the researchers discovered that the thumb length and gender can affect the characteristics of touchscreen gestures on smartphones. The authors of [25] capture the touchscreen gestures of 62 children and 38 adults to show that a touchscreen gesture of a child can be detected with 96.6% accuracy.

One of the key aspects of touchscreen gestures that make them an optimal candidate for continuous authentication (on devices requiring touchscreen gestures to operate) is that they are frequent during the device usage (one gesture every 3.9 seconds when reading) [44] and are difficult for attackers to mimic due to behavioural features such as pressure and speed being difficult to replicate even if observed [18]. One seminal work proposing touchscreen gestures as a behavioural biometric for continuous authentication was the *Touchalytics* study [44]. This study collected a controlled dataset of gestures on mobile devices from 41 users as they played a game requiring swipe gestures. The work proposed a unique set of 30 features that were extracted from each gesture and classified using k-NN and SVM techniques, achieving EERs ranging from 0 to 4%. Several interesting observations were also made. Firstly, authenticating single gestures could be unstable and utilising multiple gestures to form a decision can improve the EERs. Secondly, authentication difficulty can increase as the temporal distance from the training phase grows.

In [104], the authors conduct a study to assess which classifiers most optimally classify touchscreen gestures. The authors collect their own controlled dataset from 190 users, pre-process it by removing gestures of less than four touch events, and subsequently extract a set of 28 custom features. They find Logistic Regression, SVM, and Random Forest classifiers perform most accurately, giving EERs as low as 10.5%. However, different screen and gesture orientation yielded different EERs. In most of the early implementations of touchscreen gesture authentication, the primary classifiers used are two-class classifiers in which the classifier uses both genuine and impostor training data. Of course, this may not be feasible (due to scale or privacy) in the real world, and consequently some research has investigated one-class classification techniques. In [72], an investigation is conducted into one-class classifiers when applied to touchscreen gestures with findings indicating they might achieve similar accuracies as two-class approaches. It has also been shown that aspects such as the user's posture and the device size have an impact on the performance of touchscreen gesture authentication systems [119]. The touchscreen gesture can be considered a relatively continuous biometric on smartphones and

---

[5] https://developer.android.com/reference/android/view/MotionEvent.

tablets because it is a primary means of interaction (with taps and one-finger sliding accounting for 98% of all gestures [108]). However, there are still accuracy improvements that can be made.

4.4.2.4 Gesture-Typing

The concept of *gesture-typing* (also known as *swipe-typing* [114]) is a method of typing words by swiping a finger across letters on a touchscreen to form a *word-gesture* that is converted into a textual word. This form of typing words has been shown as faster than tapping each individual letter separately [93]. Creating a word-gesture requires a user to place a finger on the first letter of the word on the on-screen keyboard and slide it to each subsequent different letter in the word until the last letter is reached, at which point the finger is lifted from the keyboard and the gesture input is processed to derive the word. Gesture-typing is a relatively new concept with *Android* devices implementing a gesture-typing capable keyboard in the early 2010s. Now, by default, many touchscreen keyboards now include a gesture-typing option (including the default keyboards of *Android* and *iPhone* smartphones). Gesture-typing keyboards have a tolerance for error (a finger need not explicitly reach a letter in the word for the word to be recognised) [130], compared to tap-to-type keyboards (where a tap on an incorrect key may create a wholly different word).

In essence, a word-gesture is fundamentally a touchscreen gesture (explored in Sect. 4.4.2.3). The same vector of touch events (commonly consisting of x and y coordinates, area, pressure, and timestamp values) is generated when a word-gesture is performed on the touchscreen. However, word-gestures carry specific nuances (due to the swiping between different letters) that touchscreen gestures (such as single swipes and scrolls) do not. These nuances may include multiple points within the gesture at which the finger performs a redirection (identifiable by angle) and/or a pause (identifiable by the decrease in speed). These nuances do not lend themselves well to traditional touchscreen gesture features, such as those in [44], because such features were designed for a smooth trajectory between two points. For example, a feature representing the mid-flow speed of a gesture may not be as relevant in a word-gesture made up of multiple sub-gestures between letters.

The use of gesture-typing within continuous authentication schemes is limited. This is possibly because gesture-typing is a relatively recent biometric. In 2014 a study was published that detailed a scheme for continuously authenticating users based on the words input via gesture-typing [23]. The scheme gathered words input via gesture-typing from 16 users. They extracted a subset of the touchscreen features in [44] and trained SVM classifiers for each word. They achieved EERs between 2 and 50%. However, that the system needed to be explicitly trained on a word to authenticate it makes it *word-dependent*, limiting the real-world practicality. In [114], a *word-independent* system was created by producing multiple feature groupings designed for describing the word-independent properties of word-gestures. The feature groupings described pause points, redirect points, whole-word gestures, sub-gestures, accelerometer data, and gyroscope data. The study showed that for uncontrolled text input by 20 users, the EER is 3.58% for single word-gestures and 0.81% when three word-gestures were used to authenticate. Of course, these studies have been applied only to smartphones. However, gesture-typing keyboards also exist on tablet devices which have similar capabilities to smartphones and contain similar sensors, so it is feasible to expect similar schemes to work on tablet devices.

4.4.2.5   Eye Movement

The human eye is capable of four different types of basic movement; these are eye saccades, smooth pursuit movements, vergence movements, and vestibulo-ocular movements [54]. The eye *saccade* is the quick and sudden movement of the eyes between two fixed points of focus and can occur up to 173,000 times a day [2]. Saccades allow the central part of the retina, the fovea (which provides only a small high-resolution window of our vision of about $1°$ [107]), to quickly shift focus. The movement is so rapid (up to $700°/s$ [56]) that the saccade-generating system cannot take into account changes in the target position and requires a new saccade to correct the position [54]. These movements occur as a result of six extraocular muscles which are controlled by lower motor neurons that form three cranial nerves [54]. The points of focus between eye saccades are known as *fixations* [132] and usually last for 200–300 ms [68]. Recent studies have shown that eye saccades and fixations, shown in Fig. 4.2, can reveal individual personality [58] and even identity [68].

Systems that utilise eye movement for biometric authentication typically consist of three components. The first is the presentation of one or more stimuli (such as text or video) to elicit eye movement, the second is an eye tracker (either head-mounted or remote), and the third is a gaze descriptor (which models the eye movements for classification) [48]. One early study investigating eye movement as a biometric was done in 2004 [68]. The authors used an infrared-based system to track eye movements whilst an on-screen dot moved between a 3×3 grid. Features were extracted from the eye movements via cepstral coefficients and classified using k-Nearest Neighbours to achieve a FAR of 1.48% and a FRR of 22.59%. This approach, however, was not continuous and required intrusive stimulus.

Recent studies have shown that eye movements can also be utilised for continuous authentication. In [56], the authors attempt to identify scanpath (sequences of saccades and fixations) features that may be used as a biometric indicator. A screen placed 685 mm from 32 participants displayed excerpts from Lewis Carroll's *The Hunting of the Snark* whilst a tracking system (collecting at 1000 Hz) collected eye movements. Features (e.g., average fixation duration and average vectorial saccade amplitude) were extracted such that the user similarity scores could be computed and fused via a weighted mean, achieving an EER of 27%. In [57], the authors follow up this study with the same methodology. This time they use eye movements collected via tracking systems at high resolution (1000 Hz) and at low resolution

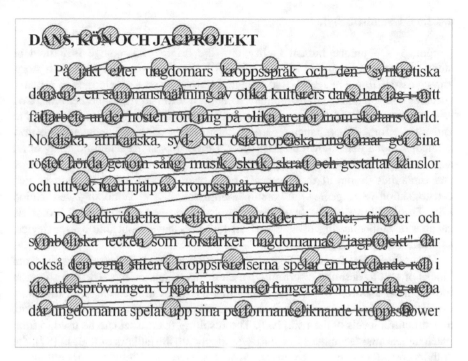

Fig. 4.2 Showing the eye saccades as lines between points of fixation for an individual reading text. This would be expected to differ for different individuals (Source: WikiMedia Commons)

(75 Hz) and a smaller feature set. The lowest EER of 16.5% was achieved via using a Random Forest on all individual feature comparisons on the high-resolution data.

In [37], a continuous eye movement authentication scheme designed to stop attacks on PCs from insiders with system knowledge is presented. Eyes of users were tracked at 500 Hz and three feature groups were extracted, including (i) pupil features (based on pupil diameter), (ii) temporal features (based on saccades and fixations), and (iii) spatial features (based on gaze steadiness). Using all 21 features with an SVM achieved an EER of 3.98% during the same session, 6.05% for sessions an hour apart, and 7.37% for sessions 2 weeks apart. They detected up to 92.2% of attackers within 40 seconds. A follow-up study in [36] found, in optimal conditions, an EER of 1.88% could be achieved. The study also shows EERs increase when trained and tested on eye movements from non-matching tasks (e.g., reading and browsing). Using eye movements to authenticate has advantages over mouse movement and keyboard dynamics because they are more frequent [37]. Compared to iris biometrics, eye movements are not currently as accurate but are more difficult to spoof. Spoofing eye movements would require an attacker to produce artificial moving eyes and obtain accurate real-world eye movement data from the genuine user [36].

4.4.2.6   Linguistic Style

Language is a unique human ability and the origin of language is a field of study that remains engulfed in mystery [126]. The Book of Genesis tells a story, known as the *Tower of Babel*, that languages arose when a single race of humans speaking the same language attempted to build a tower to reach the heavens, God saw this and scattered the humans around the world with different languages to end their efforts. These languages and the nuances of these languages are now studied within a field known as *linguistics*. Linguistics is the scientific study of all aspects of human language, including phonetics, phonology, morphology, syntax, and semantics. Some of these aspects have been studied for tasks such as text categorisation (e.g., genre), authorship identification, and authorship verification [99]. The last few decades have seen linguistics used as a behavioural biometric capable of authenticating users based on text they have input into a user device, such as an SMS message [97].

Using linguistics for continuous authentication relies on features extracted from blocks of text to describe discriminative elements of authorship. The investigation into optimal features to describe linguistics has been a research topic for many decades [49]. However, common features are often obtained at the lexical, syntactic, and structural levels of the text [100]. The resulting feature set can be used to train machine learning techniques to identify/authenticate the authors of text. In [97], the authors consider linguistic profiling of SMS messages as a biometric for continuous authentication and utilise word profiling, lexical, syntactic, and structural features. They present an SMS-based linguistic continuous authentication scheme. Their scheme implemented a neural network to assess the messages of 30 users and achieved an average EER of 24%. The authors follow up this study in [99] and [100], in which they use their linguistic approach in a continuous authentication scheme and achieve average EERs as low as 16.4% (when optimal features are selected for each user).

In [87], the authors propose a system for continuous linguistic authentication using one-class isolation forest classifiers. In order to improve the frequency, the system can authenticate they use smaller blocks of text than other studies, using 50 and 100 characters for the analysis. They achieve accuracies of 90%+ when testing their scheme on the blog entries of 1,000 users. Linguistics are a simple biometric to collect, requiring only a keyboard, which is available on most user devices (laptops, tablets, smartphones, etc.). They have also been shown to have a level of permanence with indications of consistency in linguistic style over time [87]. However, whilst linguistic biometrics can provide discriminating characteristics, their responsiveness is limited due to a requirement to obtain a block of text for the analysis.

4.4.2.7   Gait

The term *gait* refers to the pattern of movements made when walking. Throughout the history gait analysis has been a subject of interest with early examples dating back to 350 BC with Aristotle's *De Motu Animalium* (On the Gait of Animals), in which he questioned and analysed the gait of different animals [12]. Some animals (such as most ungulates) are *precocial* and can walk soon after birth [73]; there are evolutionary benefits for this because a newborn may otherwise be easy prey [89]. However, humans are an *altricial* organism and walking is a behaviour that is gradually learned over a time period [89]. The process of learning to walk is fraught with attempts to walk (with toddlers falling on average 17 times per hour) that ultimately leads to successful walking [89]. In humans the pattern of walking results from a complex process involving the brain, spinal cord, peripheral nerves, muscles, bones, and joints [127]. The individual gait resulting from this process has been shown to have distinct properties that can be used to recognise and identify individuals.

Gait is sometimes seen as advantageous because it does not necessarily need close user proximity to be collected (it has a high *stand-off distance*) [64]. There are therefore multiple ways gait can be collected: (i) machine vision (MV), in which cameras are used to capture walking (ii) floor sensor (FS), where floor sensors measure walking force and frequency, and (iii) wearable sensors (WSs), where the user wears a sensor [47]. However, the approaches using gait for continuous authentication will usually be implemented on user devices worn by the user (or at least on the body of the user). These often utilise accelerometer sensors to capture gait movement as frequently sampled x, y, and z readings representing tri-axis acceleration. This accelerometer data is then used to derive features such as *gait-cycle-based* features [requiring the detection of a single gait cycle (often two steps) and forming an average template] and *frame-based* features (statistical features from frames of sensor data) [125]. The features (after possible pre-processing) can be used with distance-based or machine learning classification approaches to assess gait similarities [125].

Modern user devices that would be expected to be on a user's person to facilitate gait recognition include wearables and smartphones. The accelerometers in mobile devices have motivated gait recognition research, and in [135] the authors propose a pace independent gait algorithm that is insensitive to variability in walking speed to counteract real-world gait variation. They use gait dynamics images (GDIs), an orientation invariant representation of accelerometer data, to perform their gait normalisation. In [10], the authors note that many gait recognition studies rely on datasets that are collected in controlled environments, which may lead to unrealistic performance. To remedy this the authors collect an unconstrained real-world dataset from 44 smartphone users over 7–10 days, extracting feature frames and training a Feed-Forward Multilayered Perceptron classifier. Their proposed model has achieved EERs of 11.38%, 11.32%, 24.52%, 27.33%, and 15.08% for normal, fast, down, and upstairs gait activities, respectively. Work has also been done on smartwatches (which comes with the advantage of constant placement/orientation on the body). In [5], the authors collect accelerometer and gyroscope data from the *Microsoft Band 2*, extract features from 10-second segments, and achieve EERs as low as 0.13%.

There are several considerations that must be kept in mind when producing continuous gait authentication systems. The first is that gait may be changed by footwear, walking surface, clothing, load carrying, and ageing [125]. One must also consider that gait is not a biometric that is completely universal, with it being unsuitable for those that must use a wheelchair [26]. Furthermore, because the user must walk to authenticate the device, using gait recognition alone does not provide a fully continuous authentication scheme during device usage. However, whilst gait is a visible behavioural biometric, it is difficult for impostors to mimic (not least due to the physiological differences that influence gait behaviour). In [81], the authors show that mimicry attacks are difficult to perform even when the attacker is trained, and the attackers will reach a plateau after which mimicry improvement is difficult.

4.4.2.8 Location

The capability to obtain a user's location is now a feature on many user devices, such as smartphones and smartwatches. This is mostly done via the Global Positioning System (GPS), created and operated by the United States of America. The GPS system is a collection of satellites that orbit Earth broadcasting their location such that a receiving device can compute the distance from multiple satellites and use trilateration to calculate a location (as latitude and longitude coordinates, accurate to 5–10 m). In recent continuous authentication studies, the geographical habits of the user (such as where the user is at certain times of day) have been used successfully as a behavioural biometric [46]. This is because humans are creatures of habit (most individuals frequent the same places, such as their workplace), and their location patterns are distinguishable even from those in the same city [46].

In [129], the authors show how life patterns can be mined from the location history. They propose an algorithm that clusters GPS points with regard to temporal occurrence to identify patterns such that movement behaviour and activity can be predicted. Clustering of GPS coordinates is often necessary because the coordinates are noisy and rarely identical despite being at the same location. Most studies employing location history are based on pattern mining, and few studies have used these patterns to authenticate users. The first location-only continuous authentication scheme is PATH (Person Authentication using Trace Histories) [76]. The authors model GPS points as clusters (20 m of diameter) of user movement as a Markovian motion and propose a modified Hidden Markov Model (HMM) solution such that movements can be given a verification score. Their solution is trained on up to 4 weeks of historical location data and is shown to yield an EER of 20.73%.

Employing location as a single modality offers high levels of usability because devices may be unlocked in recognised locations. However, this also results in weak levels of security against informed attackers that know the movement patterns of the genuine user. This is mitigated in schemes using location as biometric alongside other biometrics such as in [46] where the location is combined with stylometry, app usage, and browsing history. One other drawback is that GPS has been shown to be one of the biggest drains on battery life [79], which might hinder the user experience. Finally, it is also the case that a long training period is required (4 weeks in [76]), such that nuances of a geographical habits can be obtained, which leaves a window in which the authentication would not be active.

4.4.2.9 Voice

The human voice has long been known as having to carry distinctive traits for different individuals, and we are capable of accurately distinguishing different voices when listening to an audio stream of multiple individuals' talk [105]. The differences in voices are a result of a number of factors. One factor is the shape of the physical characteristics of the vocal tract, mouth, nasal cavities, and lips [64]. The differences in the shape and size of these characteristics can result in differences in tone, pitch, and resonance. Another factor is the effects of behavioural characteristics on the voice such as regional accents, cultural norms, and speech rhythm. This combination of factors results in voice biometrics being considered both physiological and behavioural [64]. Using voice biometrics to authenticate a user is commonly known as *speaker recognition*, as the goal is to recognise the speaker.

Many different user devices have a microphone built into them these days, including smartphones, tablets, laptops, and smartwatches. This enables functionality for calls, message dictation, voice notes, and voice assistants (e.g., *Siri*). Continuous authentication can make use of the microphone to perform speaker recognition. This might be done each time a voice feature is explicitly used or each time a voice is heard. There are two ways speaker recognition can be implemented [78]. The first is known as *text-dependent* and requires that the words used during enrolment are identical to those used when wishing to authenticate. The second is known as *text-independent* and can authenticate the user even if the words used in enrolment are different from those used to authenticate. The latter technique is more practical for continuous authentication because it is less restrictive, but the former is often more accurate as matches between the same words can be more robust [3].

An early study detailing a text-independent continuous voice-based authentication system for smartphones known as *SpeakerSense* was published in 2011 [75]. Conscious of the potential degradation on device resources (e.g., battery life) of such a system, the authors gave focus to the efficient running of the system through only activating an energy-intensive speaker recognition module if a low-power module detected there is speech. The speaker recognition module utilises MFCCs (Mel-frequency cepstral coefficients) which are extracted and classified with Gaussian Mixture Models (GMMs). They conduct a study on 17 users and achieve an accuracy of 98%. Another study also produced a text-independent speaker authentication scheme for smartphones [122]. The system gave special attention to real-world usage and therefore collected voice data from both noisy and quiet environments. They applied a voice activity detection module to identify voice events and then extracted LPCCs (Linear Prediction Cepstral Coefficients) which were classified with a Naïve Bayes classifier. They achieved an accuracy of

92% in quiet environments and a lower 82% in noisy environments (as would be expected).

One recent system was designed for authenticating interactions with voice assistants via wearable technology (e.g., glasses) [41]. The system used an electronic wearable device designed to collect body-surface vibrations when the user speaks, then matching it with the speech signal received by the voice assistant. The benefit of this is that attacks that replay a voice command to a voice assistant would not work without the matching vibration signal from the wearable device. However, the requirement to regularly have a wearable device on the user may hinder usability and convenience. Employing speaker recognition within continuous biometric authentication systems has limitations. This is because the voice is not always a continuous or even frequent modality and may not be present during device use. Furthermore, in some situations where the voice is present, the environmental noise can degrade authentication accuracies [122]. The voice is also susceptible to behavioural variation and can change significantly due to environment or illness [64]. Lastly, authentication mechanisms that utilise voice biometrics must also be aware of the potential attacks in which a genuine voice is replayed, mimicked, or synthesised [80].

4.5   Multibiometrics

One popular application of multibiometrics within recent continuous authentication works is in creating multi-modal systems. These take advantage of recent sensor-dense user devices, allowing for multiple biometric modalities to be collected. However, the use of multi-modal biometrics in continuous authentication system is still relatively new. In a 2016 study it was noted that in a survey of such systems, only 30% employed multi-modal biometrics [4]. The advantages of multi-modal biometrics are numerous. Compared with *unimodal* systems, multi-modal biometric systems can expect better protection from spoof attacks, higher recognition rates, less affected by environmental factors, and increased robustness and reliability [96]. As discussed in Sect. 3.5.4, biometric fusion can occur at different levels. The preferred practice is to fuse the multi-modal biometrics at the score level [55]. This level does not have the rigidity of fusing at the decision-level and is not affected by the potential feature incompatibilities of fusion at the extraction level [63]. In multi-modal systems the approach should (1) account for the reliability of different modalities, (2) discount older observations from modalities, and (3) handle lack of observations from one or more modalities upon fusion [111]. Furthermore, it is noted that multi-modal approaches perform better when modalities are uncorrelated [94].

In 2011, a multi-modal system was produced to authenticate smartphone users based on their telephone, SMS, browser, and location data [110]. They collected these behavioural modalities over a period of two weeks from more than 50 subjects. They utilised score-level fusion, employing weighted sum and product fusion approaches. A study in 2012 proposed a similar idea of a multi-modal continuous authentication system for smartphones [98]. In their approach they used linguistic style, keystroke dynamics, and messaging behaviours. These modalities were fused at the score level using sum and weighted average fusion approaches. They achieved an EER of 8%. The authors expand this work with another multi-modal system in [100] and report a lower EER of 3.3%. A system for authenticating during e-learning was proposed in [42]. They use a multi-modal approach with a mixture of physiological and behavioural biometric modalities. They use face, voice, keystroke dynamics, and touchscreen gestures. The fusion takes place at the score level with weighted sum score fusion. However, no implementation details or results are provided.

In [45], a continuous biometric authentication system was developed for office computers, utilising mouse movements, mouse clicks, scroll wheel events, and keystroke events. These modalities were collected from 67 users, whilst they worked in an office environment for a period of a week. They used 60% of the data for training and developed a parallel binary decision-level fusion architecture to fuse the modalities. The system was able to authenticate with a FAR of 0.4% and a FRR of 1% after 30 seconds, though with 5 minutes of data this decreased to below 0.1% and 0.2%, respectively. In a follow-up study the decision-level fusion architecture is used to produce a continuous biometric authentication system for smartphones [46]. The modalities used in this system include stylometry, application usage, web browsing, and location data. They collected these modalities from the smartphones of 200 users for a period of at least 30 days. This system achieved an EER of 5% when 1 minute of data had been used to authenticate. This dropped to an EER of 1% when 30 minutes of data was used (though this improvement in performance could create an attack window for 30 minutes before the user is authenticated).

Another smartphone multi-modal system is proposed in [69] in which models are constructed for different spatial and temporal contexts. They built profiles from sensor data such as that of Wi-Fi networks, cell towers, application use, light, sound, and device statistics. The authors demonstrate the impostor detection rates based on impostors with differing knowledge of the user's routine. These rates ranged from 53 to 99% depending on the impostor type. The scores for each modality were fused via a simple average. A similar multi-modal approach also built different models from data collected in different spatial and temporal contexts [113]. Their approach utilised a score-level fusion strategy in which uncertainty (computed based on the accuracy and quality of each modality) was incorporated via the Dempster–Shafer theory. The approach achieved an EER as low as 9.94%, significantly lower than the 31.42% achieved from simply averaging the scores. Overall, it is indicated in the literature that there are a variety of benefits to multibiometric systems.

4.6 Summary

This chapter provided an in-depth review of the concept of biometrics and how some biometrics can be used within a continuous biometric authentication system. Firstly, the need for biometrics that can be collected in a continuous manner is discussed. The common biometric requirements (e.g., permanence, universality, distinctiveness, etc.) for selecting biometrics are next described. The types of biometric functionality (identification or verification) are then discussed. Then the different types of modalities (both physiological and behavioural) were explored and described within the context of continuous biometric authentication. Lastly, the use of these biometrics in a multibiometric (e.g., multi-modal) system was discussed.

References

1. Abate, A.F., Nappi, M., Ricciardi, S.: I-am: Implicitly authenticate me—person authentication on mobile devices through ear shape and arm gesture. IEEE Trans. Syst. Man Cybernet. Syst. **49**(3), 469–481 (2019)
2. Abrams, R., Meyer, D., Kornblum, S.: Speed and accuracy of saccadic eye movements: characteristics of impulse variability in the oculomotor system. J. Experimen. Psychol. Human Percept. Perform. **15**, 529–43 (1989)
3. Abuhamad, M., Abusnaina, A., Nyang, D., Mohaisen, D.: Sensor-based continuous authentication of smartphones' users using behavioral biometrics: a contemporary survey. IEEE Int. Things J. **8**(1), 65–84 (2021)
4. Al Abdulwahid, A., Clarke, N., Stengel, I., Furnell, S., Reich, C.: Continuous and transparent multimodal authentication: reviewing the state of the art. Cluster Comput. **19**(1), 455–474 (2016)
5. Al-Naffakh, N., Clarke, N., Li, F., Haskell-Dowland, P.: Unobtrusive gait recognition using smartwatches. In: 2017 International Conference of the Biometrics Special Interest Group (BIOSIG), pp. 1–5 (2017)
6. Al Solami, E., Boyd, C., Clark, A., Islam, A.K.: Continuous biometric authentication: Can it be more practical? In: 2010 IEEE 12th International Conference on High Performance Computing and Communications (HPCC), pp. 647–652 (2010)
7. AlGhatrif, M., Lindsay, J.: A brief review: history to understand fundamentals of electrocardiography. J. Commun. Hosp. Intern. Med. Perspect. **2**(1), (2012). https://doi.org/10.3402/jchimp.v2i1.14383. 23882360[pmid]
8. Ali Fahmi, P., Kodirov, E., Choi, D.J., Lee, G.S., Mohd Fikri Azli, A., Sayeed, S.: Implicit authentication based on ear shape biometrics using smartphone camera during a call. In: 2012 IEEE International Conference on Systems, Man, and Cybernetics (SMC), pp. 2272–2276 (2012)
9. Almalki, S., Chatterjee, P., Roy, K.: Continuous authentication using mouse clickstream data analysis. In: Security, Privacy, and Anonymity in Computation, Communication, and Storage: SpaCCS 2019 International Workshops, Atlanta, GA, USA, July 14–17, 2019, Proceedings 12, pp. 76–85. Springer, Berlin (2019)
10. Alobaidi, H., Clarke, N., Li, F., Alruban, A.: Real-world smartphone-based gait recognition. Comput. Security **113**, 102557 (2022)
11. Antal, M., Bokor, Z., Szabó, L.Z.: Information revealed from scrolling interactions on mobile devices. Pattern Recog. Lett. **56**, 7–13 (2015)
12. Aristotle: On the Gait of Animals. Kessinger Publishing, Whitefish (2004)

13. Arteaga-Falconi, J.S., Al Osman, H., El Saddik, A.: ECG authentication for mobile devices. IEEE Trans. Instrument. Measurem. **65**(3), 591–600 (2016)
14. Ayotte, B., Banavar, M., Hou, D., Schuckers, S.: Fast free-text authentication via instance-based keystroke dynamics. IEEE Trans. Biometr. Behavior Ident. Sci. **2**(4), 377–387 (2020)
15. Bertillon, A.: La photographie judiciaire: avec un appendice sur la classification et l'identification anthropométriques. Gauthier-Villars, Paris (1890)
16. Bertillon, A., McClaughry, R.W.: Signaletic Instructions Including the Theory and Practice of Anthropometrical Identification. Werner Company, Itasca (1896)
17. Betts, J.G., Desaix, P., Johnson, E.: Anatomy and Physiology. OpenStax, Houston (2013)
18. Bevan, C., Fraser, D.S.: Different strokes for different folks? Revealing the physical characteristics of smartphone users from their swipe gestures. Int. J. Human-Comput. Stud. **88**, 51–61 (2016)
19. Biel, L., Pettersson, O., Philipson, L., Wide, P.: Ecg analysis: a new approach in human identification. IEEE Trans. Instrum. Meas. **50**(3), 808–812 (2001)
20. Bonissi, A., Labati, R.D., Perico, L., Sassi, R., Scotti, F., Sparagino, L.: A preliminary study on continuous authentication methods for photoplethysmography biometrics. In: 2013 IEEE Workshop on Biometric Measurements and Systems for Security and Medical Applications, pp. 28–33 (2013)
21. Bours, P., Barghouthi, H.: Continuous authentication using biometric keystroke dynamics. In: The Norwegian Information Security Conference (NISK), vol. 2009, pp. 1–12 (2009)
22. Buker, A.A.N., Roffo, G., Vinciarelli, A.: Type like a man! inferring gender from keystroke dynamics in live-chats. IEEE Intell. Syst. **34**(6), 53–59 (2019)
23. Burgbacher, U., Hinrichs, K.: An implicit author verification system for text messages based on gesture typing biometrics. In: Proceedings of the SIGCHI Conference on Human Factors in Computing Systems, CHI '14, p. 2951–2954. Association for Computing Machinery, New York (2014)
24. Camara, C., Peris-Lopez, P., Gonzalez-Manzano, L., Tapiador, J.: Real-time electrocardiogram streams for continuous authentication. Appl. Soft Comput. **68**, 784–794 (2018)
25. Cheng, Y., Ji, X., Li, X., Zhang, T., Malebary, S., Qu, X., Xu, W.: Identifying child users via touchscreen interactions. ACM Trans. Sen. Netw. **16**(4), 1–25 (2020)
26. Clarke, N.: Transparent User Authentication: Biometrics, RFID and Behavioural Profiling, 1st edn. Springer Publishing Company, New York (2011)
27. Clarke, N.L., Furnell, S.M.: Authenticating mobile phone users using keystroke analysis. Int. J. Inf. Secur. **6**(1), 1–14 (2007)
28. Clarke, N., Karatzouni, S., Furnell, S.: Transparent facial recognition for mobile devices. In: Proceedings of the 7th Security Conference, pp. 1–13 (2008)
29. Cook, H.I., Harrison, K., James, H.: Individuals lacking ridge detail: a case study in adermatoglyphia. J. For. Sci. **66**(1), 202–208 (2021)
30. Crawford, H.: Keystroke dynamics: Characteristics and opportunities. In: 2010 Eighth International Conference on Privacy, Security and Trust, pp. 205–212 (2010)
31. Crouse, D., Han, H., Chandra, D., Barbello, B., Jain, A.K.: Continuous authentication of mobile user: Fusion of face image and inertial measurement unit data. In: 2015 International Conference on Biometrics (ICB), pp. 135–142 (2015)
32. da Silva, H.P., Fred, A., Lourenço, A., Jain, A.K.: Finger ECG signal for user authentication: Usability and performance. In: 2013 IEEE Sixth International Conference on Biometrics: Theory, Applications and Systems (BTAS), pp. 1–8 (2013)
33. Daugman, J.: Statistical demands of identification versus verification. https://www.cl.cam.ac.uk/~jgd1000/veri/veri.html
34. Daugman, J.: How iris recognition works. IEEE Trans. Circuits Syst. Video Technol. **14**(1), 21–30 (2004)
35. Eberz, S., Paoletti, N., Roeschlin, M., Kwiatkowska, M., Martinovic, I., Patané, A.: Broken hearted: How to attack ECG biometrics. In: Network and Distributed System Security Symposium 2017 (2017)

36. Eberz, S., Lovisotto, G., Rasmussen, K.B., Lenders, V., Martinovic, I.: 28 blinks later: Tackling practical challenges of eye movement biometrics. In: Proceedings of the 2019 ACM SIGSAC Conference on Computer and Communications Security, CCS '19, pp. 1187–1199. Association for Computing Machinery, New York (2019)

37. Eberz, S., Rasmussen, K.B., Lenders, V., Martinovic, I.: Preventing lunchtime attacks: Fighting insider threats with eye movement biometrics. In: 22nd Annual Network and Distributed System Security Symposium, NDSS 2015, San Diego, California, USA, February 8–11, 2014. The Internet Society, Reston (2015)

38. Eglitis, T., Guest, R., Deravi, F.: Data behind mobile behavioural biometrics – a survey. IET Biom. **9**, 224–237(13) (2020)

39. Engelbart, D.C.: XY position indicator for a display system. US Patent **3**(541), 541 (1970)

40. Fathy, M.E., Patel, V.M., Chellappa, R.: Face-based active authentication on mobile devices. In: 2015 IEEE International Conference on Acoustics, Speech and Signal Processing (ICASSP), pp. 1687–1691 (2015)

41. Feng, H., Fawaz, K., Shin, K.G.: Continuous authentication for voice assistants. In: Proceedings of the 23rd Annual International Conference on Mobile Computing and Networking, MobiCom '17, p. 343–355. Association for Computing Machinery, New York (2017)

42. Fenu, G., Marras, M., Boratto, L.: A multi-biometric system for continuous student authentication in e-learning platforms. Pattern Recogn. Lett. **113**, 83–92 (2018). Integrating Biometrics and Forensics

43. Fierrez, J., Pozo, A., Martinez-Diaz, M., Galbally, J., Morales, A.: Benchmarking touchscreen biometrics for mobile authentication. IEEE Trans. Inf. Forensics Secur. **13**(11), 2720–2733 (2018)

44. Frank, M., Biedert, R., Ma, E., Martinovic, I., Song, D.: Touchalytics: on the applicability of touchscreen input as a behavioral biometric for continuous authentication. IEEE Trans. Inf. Forensics Secur. **8**(1), 136–148 (2013)

45. Fridman, L., Stolerman, A., Acharya, S., Brennan, P., Juola, P., Greenstadt, R., Kam, M.: Multi-modal decision fusion for continuous authentication. Comput. Electr. Eng. **41**, 142–156 (2015)

46. Fridman, L., Weber, S., Greenstadt, R., Kam, M.: Active authentication on mobile devices via stylometry, application usage, web browsing, and GPS location. IEEE Syst. J. **11**(2), 513–521 (2017)

47. Gafurov, D.: A survey of biometric gait recognition: Approaches, security and challenges. In: Annual Norwegian Computer Science Conference, pp. 19–21. Annual Norwegian Computer Science Conference Norway (2007)

48. Galdi, C., Nappi, M., Riccio, D., Wechsler, H.: Eye movement analysis for human authentication: a critical survey. Pattern Recogn. Lett. **84**, 272–283 (2016)

49. Gamon, M.: Linguistic correlates of style: Authorship classification with deep linguistic analysis features. International Conference on Computational Linguistics (2004)

50. Gao, Y., Wang, W., Phoha, V.V., Sun, W., Jin, Z.: EarEcho: Using ear canal echo for wearable authentication. Proc. ACM Interact. Mob. Wearable Ubiquitous Technol. **3**(3), 1–24 (2019)

51. Gunetti, D., Picardi, C.: Keystroke analysis of free text. ACM Trans. Inf. Syst. Secur. **8**(3), 312–347 (2005)

52. Gunetti, D., Picardi, C., Ruffo, G.: Dealing with different languages and old profiles in keystroke analysis of free text. In: Proceedings of the 9th Conference on Advances in Artificial Intelligence, AI*IA'05, p. 347–358. Springer, Berlin (2005)

53. Haasnoot, E., Barnhoorrr, J., Spreeuwers, L., Veldhuis, R., Verwey, W.: Towards understanding the effects of practice on behavioural biometric recognition performance. In: 2018 26th European Signal Processing Conference (EUSIPCO), pp. 558–562 (2018)

54. Halterman, M.W.: Neuroscience, 3rd edition. Neurology **64**(4), 769–769–a (2005)

55. He, M., Horng, S.J., Fan, P., Run, R.S., Chen, R.J., Lai, J.L., Khan, M.K., Sentosa, K.O.: Performance evaluation of score level fusion in multimodal biometric systems. Pattern Recogn. **43**(5), 1789–1800 (2010)

56. Holland, C., Komogortsev, O.V.: Biometric identification via eye movement scanpaths in reading. In: 2011 International Joint Conference on Biometrics (IJCB), pp. 1–8 (2011)
57. Holland, C.D., Komogortsev, O.V.: Complex eye movement pattern biometrics: Analyzing fixations and saccades. In: 2013 International Conference on Biometrics (ICB), pp. 1–8 (2013)
58. Hoppe, S., Loetscher, T., Morey, S.A., Bulling, A.: Eye movements during everyday behavior predict personality traits. Front. Hum. Neurosci. **12**, 105 (2018)
59. Huang, J., Hou, D., Schuckers, S., Law, T., Sherwin, A.: Benchmarking keystroke authentication algorithms. In: 2017 IEEE Workshop on Information Forensics and Security (WIFS), pp. 1–6 (2017)
60. Hurley, D.J., Arbab-Zavar, B., Nixon, M.S.: The ear as a biometric. In: 2007 15th European Signal Processing Conference, pp. 25–29. IEEE, Piscataway (2007)
61. Ingale, M., Cordeiro, R., Thentu, S., Park, Y., Karimian, N.: ECG biometric authentication: a comparative analysis. IEEE Access **8**, 117853–117866 (2020)
62. Jain, A.K., Ross, A., Prabhakar, S.: An introduction to biometric recognition. IEEE Trans. Circuits Syst. Video Technol. **14**(1), 4–20 (2004)
63. Jain, A., Nandakumar, K., Ross, A.: Score normalization in multimodal biometric systems. Pattern Recogn. **38**(12), 2270–2285 (2005)
64. Jain, A.K., Ross, A.A., Nandakumar, K.: Introduction to Biometrics. Springer Publishing Company, New York (2011)
65. Jiangyu, L., Yinggang, X., Hui, W., Guangjun, L.: A face recognition system based on improved convolutional neural network. In: Proceedings of the 2019 2nd International Conference on Algorithms, Computing and Artificial Intelligence, ACAI '19, pp. 230–235. Association for Computing Machinery, New York (2020)
66. Kahn, D.: The Codebreakers: The Story of Secret Writing. Macmillan, New York (1967)
67. Kanwisher, N., McDermott, J., Chun, M.M.: The fusiform face area: a module in human extrastriate cortex specialized for face perception. J. Neurosci. **17**(11), 4302–4311 (1997). https://doi.org/10.1523/JNEUROSCI.17-11-04302.1997
68. Kasprowski, P., Ober, J.: Eye movements in biometrics. In: Maltoni, D., Jain, A.K. (eds.) Biometric Authentication, pp. 248–258. Springer, Berlin (2004)
69. Kayacik, H.G., Just, M., Baillie, L., Aspinall, D., Micallef, N.: Data driven authentication: On the effectiveness of user behaviour modelling with mobile device sensors (2014). Preprint arXiv:1410.7743
70. Klosterman, A.J., Ganger, G.R.: Secure continuous biometric-enhanced authentication (CMU-CS-00-134) (2001)
71. Korshunov, P., Marcel, S.: Vulnerability assessment and detection of deepfake videos. In: 2019 International Conference on Biometrics (ICB), pp. 1–6 (2019)
72. Kumar, R., Kundu, P.P., Phoha, V.V.: Continuous authentication using one-class classifiers and their fusion. In: 2018 IEEE 4th International Conference on Identity, Security, and Behavior Analysis (ISBA), pp. 1–8 (2018)
73. Leliveld, L.M.C.: From science to practice: a review of laterality research on ungulate livestock. Symmetry **11**(9), 1157 (2019)
74. Lu, C., Tang, X.: Surpassing human-level face verification performance on LFW with Gaussian face. In: Proceedings of the Twenty-Ninth AAAI Conference on Artificial Intelligence, AAAI'15, p. 3811–3819. AAAI Press, Washington (2015)
75. Lu, H., Bernheim Brush, A., Priyantha, B., Karlson, A.K., Liu, J.: SpeakerSense: Energy efficient unobtrusive speaker identification on mobile phones. In: Pervasive Computing: 9th International Conference, Pervasive 2011, San Francisco, USA, June 12–15, 2011. Proceedings 9, pp. 188–205. Springer, Berlin (2011)
76. Mahbub, U., Chellappa, R.: Path: Person authentication using trace histories. In: 2016 IEEE 7th Annual Ubiquitous Computing, Electronics Mobile Communication Conference (UEMCON), pp. 1–8 (2016)

77. Mahbub, U., Patel, V.M., Chandra, D., Barbello, B., Chellappa, R.: Partial face detection for continuous authentication. In: 2016 IEEE International Conference on Image Processing (ICIP), pp. 2991–2995 (2016)
78. Meng, W., Wong, D.S., Furnell, S., Zhou, J.: Surveying the development of biometric user authentication on mobile phones. IEEE Commun. Surveys Tutor. **17**(3), 1268–1293 (2015)
79. Micallef, N., Kayacık, H.G., Just, M., Baillie, L., Aspinall, D.: Sensor use and usefulness: Trade-offs for data-driven authentication on mobile devices. In: 2015 IEEE International Conference on Pervasive Computing and Communications (PerCom), pp. 189–197 (2015)
80. Mittal, A., Dua, M.: Automatic speaker verification systems and spoof detection techniques: review and analysis. Int. J. Speech Technol. **25**, 1–30 (2022)
81. Mjaaland, B.B., Bours, P., Gligoroski, D.: Walk the walk: Attacking gait biometrics by imitation. In: Burmester, M., Tsudik, G., Magliveras, S., Ilić, I. (eds.) Information Security, pp. 361–380. Springer, Berlin (2011)
82. Mock, K., Hoanca, B., Weaver, J., Milton, M.: Real-time continuous iris recognition for authentication using an eye tracker. In: Proceedings of the 2012 ACM Conference on Computer and Communications Security, CCS '12, pp. 1007–1009. Association for Computing Machinery, New York (2012)
83. Mondal, S., Bours, P.: Continuous authentication using mouse dynamics. In: 2013 International Conference of the BIOSIG Special Interest Group (BIOSIG), pp. 1–12 (2013)
84. Monrose, F., Rubin, A.: Authentication via keystroke dynamics. In: Proceedings of the 4th ACM Conference on Computer and Communications Security, CCS '97, pp. 48–56. Association for Computing Machinery, New York (1997)
85. Murphy, C., Huang, J., Hou, D., Schuckers, S.: Shared dataset on natural human-computer interaction to support continuous authentication research. In: 2017 IEEE International Joint Conf. on Biometrics (IJCB), pp. 525–530 (2017)
86. Nagrani, A., Albanie, S., Zisserman, A.: Seeing voices and hearing faces: Cross-modal biometric matching. In: Proceedings of the IEEE Conference on Computer Vision and Pattern Recognition (CVPR) (2018)
87. Neal, T., Sundararajan, K., Woodard, D.: Exploiting linguistic style as a cognitive biometric for continuous verification. In: 2018 International Conference on Biometrics (ICB), pp. 270–276 (2018)
88. Odinokikh, G., Korobkin, M., Solomatin, I., Efimov, I., Fartukov, A.: Iris feature extraction and matching method for mobile biometric applications. In: 2019 International Conference on Biometrics (ICB), pp. 1–6 (2019). https://doi.org/10.1109/ICB45273.2019.8987379
89. O'Mara, S.: In Praise of Walking: The New Science of How We Walk and Why It's Good for Us. Random House, New York (2019)
90. Patel, V.M., Chellappa, R., Chandra, D., Barbello, B.: Continuous user authentication on mobile devices: Recent progress and remaining challenges. IEEE Signal Process. Mag. **33**(4), 49–61 (2016)
91. Ranjan, A.: Permanence of ECG biometric: Experiments using convolutional neural networks. In: 2019 International Conference on Biometrics (ICB), pp. 1–6 (2019)
92. Revett, K., Jahankhani, H., De Magalhaes, S.T., Santos, H.M.: A survey of user authentication based on mouse dynamics. In: Global E-Security: 4th International Conference, ICGeS 2008, London, UK, June 23–25, 2008. Proceedings, pp. 210–219. Springer, Berlin (2008)
93. Reyal, S., Zhai, S., Kristensson, P.O.: Performance and User Experience of Touchscreen and Gesture Keyboards in a Lab Setting and in the Wild, pp. 679–688. Association for Computing Machinery, New York (2015)
94. Ross, A.A., Nandakumar, K., Jain, A.K.: Handbook of Multibiometrics, 1st edn. Springer Publishing Company, New York (2006)
95. Ross, A., Banerjee, S., Chen, C., Chowdhury, A., Mirjalili, V., Sharma, R., Swearingen, T., Yadav, S.: Some research problems in biometrics: The future beckons. In: 2019 International Conference on Biometrics (ICB), pp. 1–8 (2019)
96. Ryu, R., Yeom, S., Kim, S.H., Herbert, D.: Continuous multimodal biometric authentication schemes: a systematic review. IEEE Access **9**, 34541–34557 (2021)

97. Saevanee, H., Clarke, N., Furnell, S.: SMS linguistic profiling authentication on mobile device. In: 2011 5th International Conference on Network and System Security, pp. 224–228 (2011)
98. Saevanee, H., Clarke, N.L., Furnell, S.M.: Multi-modal behavioural biometric authentication for mobile devices. In: Information Security and Privacy Research: 27th IFIP TC 11 Information Security and Privacy Conference, SEC 2012, Heraklion, Crete, Greece, June 4–6, 2012. Proceedings 27, pp. 465–474. Springer, Berlin (2012)
99. Saevanee, H., Clarke, N., Furnell, S., Biscione, V.: Text-based active authentication for mobile devices. In: Cuppens-Boulahia, N., Cuppens, F., Jajodia, S., Abou El Kalam, A., Sans, T. (eds.) ICT Systems Security and Privacy Protection, pp. 99–112. Springer, Berlin (2014)
100. Saevanee, H., Clarke, N., Furnell, S., Biscione, V.: Continuous user authentication using multi-modal biometrics. Comput. Secur. **53**(C), 234–246 (2015)
101. Samangouei, P., Patel, V.M., Chellappa, R.: Attribute-based continuous user authentication on mobile devices. In: 2015 IEEE 7th International Conference on Biometrics Theory, Applications and Systems (BTAS), pp. 1–8 (2015)
102. Samangouei, P., Patel, V.M., Chellappa, R.: Facial attributes for active authentication on mobile devices. Image Vision Comput. **58**, 181–192 (2017)
103. Samarin, N., Sannella, D.: A key to your heart: Biometric authentication based on ECG signals. In: Who Are You?! Adventures in Authentication Workshop, WAY '19, pp. 1–6. Santa Clara, California, USA (2019)
104. Serwadda, A., Phoha, V.V., Wang, Z.: Which verifiers work?: A benchmark evaluation of touch-based authentication algorithms. In: 2013 IEEE Sixth International Conference on Biometrics: Theory, Applications and Systems (BTAS), pp. 1–8 (2013)
105. Sharma, N.K., Ganesh, S., Ganapathy, S., Holt, L.L.: Talker change detection: A comparison of human and machine performance. J. Acoust. Soc. Am. **145**(1), 131–142 (2019)
106. Sheehan, M.J., Nachman, M.W.: Morphological and population genomic evidence that human faces have evolved to signal individual identity. Nat. Commun. **5**(1), 4800 (2014)
107. Shelchkova, N., Poletti, M.: Modulations of foveal vision associated with microsaccade preparation. Proc. Natl. Acad. Sci. **117**(20), 11178–11183 (2020)
108. Shen, C., Li, Y., Chen, Y., Guan, X., Maxion, R.A.: Performance analysis of multi-motion sensor behavior for active smartphone authentication. IEEE Trans. Inf. Forensics Secur. **13**(1), 48–62 (2018)
109. Shepherd, S.J.: Continuous authentication by analysis of keyboard typing characteristics. In: European Convention on Security and Detection, 1995, pp. 111–114 (1995)
110. Shi, E., Niu, Y., Jakobsson, M., Chow, R.: Implicit authentication through learning user behavior. In: Information Security: 13th International Conference, ISC 2010, Boca Raton, FL, USA, October 25–28, 2010, Revised Selected Papers 13, pp. 99–113. Springer, Berlin (2011)
111. Sim, T., Zhang, S., Janakiraman, R., Kumar, S.: Continuous verification using multimodal biometrics. IEEE Trans. Pattern Anal. Mach. Intell. **29**(4), 687–700 (2007)
112. Sitová, Z., Šcděnka, J., Yang, Q., Peng, G., Zhou, G., Gasti, P., Balagani, K.S.: HMOG: New behavioral biometric features for continuous authentication of smartphone users. IEEE Trans. Inf. Forensics Secur. **11**(5), 877–892 (2016)
113. Smith-Creasey, M., Rajarajan, M.: A novel scheme to address the fusion uncertainty in multi-modal continuous authentication schemes on mobile devices. In: 2019 International Conference on Biometrics (ICB), pp. 1–8 (2019)
114. Smith-Creasey, M., Rajarajan, M.: A novel word-independent gesture-typing continuous authentication scheme for mobile devices. Comput. Secur. **83**, 140–150 (2019)
115. Smith-Creasey, M., Albalooshi, F.A., Rajarajan, M.: Context awareness for improved continuous face authentication on mobile devices. In: 2018 IEEE 16th Intl Conf on Dependable, Autonomic and Secure Computing, 16th Intl Conf on Pervasive Intelligence and Computing, 4th Intl Conf on Big Data Intelligence and Computing and Cyber Science and Technology Congress(DASC/PiCom/DataCom/CyberSciTech), pp. 644–652 (2018)

116. Smith-Creasey, M., Albalooshi, F.A., Rajarajan, M.: Continuous face authentication scheme for mobile devices with tracking and liveness detection. Microprocess. Microsyst. **63**, 147–157 (2018)
117. Spillane, R.: Keyboard apparatus for personal identification. IBM Techn. Disclosure Bull. **17**, 3346 (1975)
118. Stigler, S.M.: Galton and identification by fingerprints. Genetics **140**(3), 857 (1995)
119. Syed, Z., Helmick, J., Banerjee, S., Cukic, B.: Touch gesture-based authentication on mobile devices: the effects of user posture, device size, configuration, and inter-session variability. J. Syst. Softw. **149**, 158–173 (2019)
120. Tan, C.B.Y., Stephen, I.D., Whitehead, R., Sheppard, E.: You look familiar: how malaysian Chinese recognize faces. PLOS ONE **7**(1), 1–4 (2012)
121. Teh, P.S., Teoh, A.B.J., Yue, S.: A survey of keystroke dynamics biometrics. Sci. World J. **2013**, 408280 (2013)
122. Thullier, F., Bouchard, B., Menelas, B.A.J.: A text-independent speaker authentication system for mobile devices. Cryptography **1**(3), 16 (2017)
123. Trokielewicz, M., Czajka, A., Maciejewicz, P.: Iris recognition after death. IEEE Trans. Inf. Forensics Secur. **14**(6), 1501–1514 (2019)
124. Viola, P., Jones, M.: Rapid object detection using a boosted cascade of simple features. In: Proceedings of the 2001 IEEE Computer Society Conference on Computer Vision and Pattern Recognition. CVPR 2001, vol. 1, pp. I–I (2001)
125. Wan, C., Wang, L., Phoha, V.V.: A survey on gait recognition. ACM Comput. Surv. **51**(5), 1–35 (2018)
126. Weinert, M., et al.: On the contemporary theories of the development of human language. Acad. J. Modern Philol. (12), 229–238 (2021)
127. Whittle, M.W.: Gait Analysis: An Introduction, 3rd edn. Butterworth-Heinemann, Oxford (2005)
128. Yadav, U., Abbas, S.N., Hatzinakos, D.: Evaluation of PPG biometrics for authentication in different states. In: 2018 International Conference on Biometrics (ICB), pp. 277–282 (2018)
129. Ye, Y., Zheng, Y., Chen, Y., Feng, J., Xie, X.: Mining individual life pattern based on location history. In: 2009 Tenth International Conference on Mobile Data Management: Systems, Services and Middleware, pp. 1–10 (2009)
130. Zhai, S., Kristensson, P.O.: The word-gesture keyboard: reimagining keyboard interaction (CACM research highlight). Commun. ACM **55**(9), 91–101 (2012)
131. Zhang, K., Zhang, Z., Li, Z., Qiao, Y.: Joint face detection and alignment using multitask cascaded convolutional networks. IEEE Signal Process. Lett. **23**(10), 1499–1503 (2016)
132. Zhang, Y., Hu, W., Xu, W., Chou, C.T., Hu, J.: Continuous authentication using eye movement response of implicit visual stimuli. Proc. ACM Interact. Mob. Wearable Ubiquitous Technol. **1**(4), 1–22 (2018)
133. Zhao, T., Wang, Y., Liu, J., Chen, Y.: Your heart won't lie: PPG-based continuous authentication on wrist-worn wearable devices. In: Proceedings of the 24th Annual International Conference on Mobile Computing and Networking, MobiCom '18, p. 783–785. Association for Computing Machinery, New York (2018)
134. Zhao, T., Wang, Y., Liu, J., Chen, Y., Cheng, J., Yu, J.: Trueheart: Continuous authentication on wrist-worn wearables using PPG-based biometrics. In: IEEE INFOCOM 2020 - IEEE Conference on Computer Communications, pp. 30–39 (2020)
135. Zhong, Y., Deng, Y., Meltzner, G.: Pace independent mobile gait biometrics. In: 2015 IEEE 7th International Conference on Biometrics Theory, Applications and Systems (BTAS), pp. 1–8 (2015)

Chapter 5
Considerations and Challenges

5.1 Introduction

The field of biometrics is a well-established and mature research area with advances that have enabled us to use biometric technologies in real-world authentication solutions. These solutions come from a rich and diverse history with origins dating back to more than 100 years ago. For example, Francis Galton wrote about identification via the 'spirals and whorls' of fingerprints as early as the late 1800s [15]. The scientific progress and advancements since the earliest publications have seen the field of biometrics expand rapidly as enabled by improvements in technologies such as sensing, processing, and machine learning capabilities.

However, despite these advancements there are still important considerations and challenges that must be addressed within the field of biometrics and when they are employed within continuous biometric authentication systems. Some of these considerations arise due to the nuanced requirements that come from authenticating biometrics continuously (e.g., power usage), whereas others also are considerations that apply to any use of biometrics (e.g., attack mitigation). There have been a variety of surveys and studies discussing the challenges that face continuous biometric authentication systems and some considerations that should be addressed [30]. However, many of these considerations and challenges still persist.

5.2 Contextual Awareness

Context has been described as 'information that can be used to characterise the situation of an entity' [3]. Continuous biometric authentication systems authenticate in many contexts (e.g., based on the user activity, the environment, the time of day, or the current location). Such contexts may have a detrimental impact on biometric systems, especially if the system has not been trained on data from that context

M. Smith-Creasey, *Continuous Biometric Authentication Systems*, SpringerBriefs in Computer Science, https://doi.org/10.1007/978-3-031-49071-2_5

[29]. One approach to mitigate the effects of context that has been shown to be effective is *contextual awareness*, the functionality of a system to utilise the context to tailor information or services to a user [3]. Continuous authentication systems can therefore utilise contextual awareness to tailor the authentication approach.

The context can have a severe impact on continuous face authentication systems. In [34], a dataset of faces from 50 users in low light, indoor light, and natural light contexts was used. The study showed that different illumination contexts for training and testing degraded the authentication performance, even when histogram equalisation was applied to facial images to reduce illumination variation. The context of user activity has also been shown to effect continuous face authentication. In [41] the authors found that faces captured on smartphones during sitting, walking, and standing yield poor authentication results when different contexts are used for training and testing. In [40] a contextually aware scheme was proposed to capture user activity and illumination such that a classifier trained on data from the same context could be used to authenticate. This approach reduced EERs by around 4%.

In [29] the authors investigated the effect of context on continuous authentication systems utilising touchscreen swipe gesture interactions. The contexts were different activities on a smartphone including different types of image comparison and reading activities. The optimal performance was obtained when the touchscreen gestures used for training and testing were from the same context. Another study looked at contexts in which users were performing pre-defined reading and navigation tasks while sitting and walking [37]. The authors show that context-specific models are beneficial for different smartphone use cases and human activity scenarios in order to minimise the error rates. For example, they found that when trained on data from all contexts and tested on a reading and sitting context the EER was 25.5%, but this decreased to 11.7% when the system was trained on data from the same context.

Context can have an impact on typing. In [38] the authors investigate tap and keystroke behaviours on smartphones using features from accelerometer and gyroscope sensors in sitting and walking contexts. They find the EERs were 7.16% whilst walking and 10.05% whilst sitting. It was suggested this is due to the movement features also capturing traits of a user's gait. The context was considered in [42] where the authors authenticate gesture-typing behaviour in sitting, walking, and standing contexts using features from touchscreen-gesture, accelerometer, and gyroscope data. They show testing data from a different context to that used for training increased the EER. Contextual awareness was investigated for keystroke authentication on smartphones in [9]. The authors consider sitting, walking, and standing contexts and use gyroscope data to identify the context and select a matching classifier. This contextual awareness increased the accuracy by 30%.

It can be concluded that context can have significant effects on the biometric data collected from continuous authentication systems. These contexts may arise from numerous places, including the environmental illumination, ambient noise, physical user activity, the time of the day/week, the application used, or the current location. Sometimes biometrics from the same user but from different contexts do not match optimally (with some contexts impacting more than others) because of the effect of the context on the biometric. This can increase system error rates. Therefore, it is crucial to consider the challenges of context within a continuous authentication system and ensure that the system is able to authenticate within those contexts.

5.3 Bias

One of the primary pillars that effects trust in biometric systems is considered bias and fairness [21]. The concept of bias and fairness in biometric systems often arises due to systematic demographic biases. The literature defines a system as being demographically biased if it demonstrates significant differences in operation for different demographic groups (e.g., based on race or gender) such that certain groups are disadvantaged [11]. This mirrors human biases such as the *other-race effect*, in which individuals will recognise faces easier if they belong to the same racial group [44]. The impact of demographic bias in biometric systems can have real-world impact. It was reported in 2020 that automated UK passport checks performed poorly for certain demographics [4]. In the context of continuous authentication systems, demographic bias may, for example, increase the FRR for a certain demographic group. Such biases create unreliable and untrusted systems.

In [11] it was found that most literature studying demographic bias focused on face biometrics as the face exhibits traits such as age, gender, and race. Alarmingly, all 106 face recognition techniques from both academia and industry evaluated in the NIST Face Recognition Vendor Test (FRVT) [19] showed bias attributed to sex, age, and race because false matches increased as impostor demographic traits were made more similar. Whilst face has been a focus for demographic bias, there has also been work on bias due to factors such as age in fingerprint, finger vein, and palmprint biometrics [11]. Furthermore, traits such as beards and hairstyles have been shown to be stored in biometric face templates which can bias decisions [43].

There are multiple sources of demographic bias in biometric systems [21]. One source is due to the requirement for significant amounts of biometric training data for machine learning algorithms (especially for deep learning techniques). These large datasets regularly have an uneven distribution of demographic traits; many face recognition datasets contain faces from a disproportionately large number of white individuals which bias machine learning models [23]. Another source of bias may be derived from the biometric collection sensor not performing optimally for certain demographics (e.g., brown-eyed individuals in RGB iris recognition systems) [21].

In 2021 the *European Association for Biometrics* organised an event series focused on demographic fairness in biometric systems.[1] The authors of [33] surveyed 27 of the attending experts and reported their responses. The study reported that a majority of experts believe in the collection of large-scale biometric databases containing data from different demographics to evaluate and improve the

---

[1] https://eab.org/events/program/237.

mitigation of demographic biases in biometric systems. However, it is noted that this collection comes with privacy caveats and collection may be regulated differently within different countries. One possible solution to this is to use synthetic data (generated via GANs) that creates demographically equal datasets. However, it may be that the generated data is not sufficiently representative to reduce bias as much as genuine data.

The issue of demographic fairness is crucial to trust in biometric systems and the importance is reflected by the development of new standards (ISO/IEC WD 19795-10) that can ensure fairness. Much of the work on demographic bias has (other than face) focused on biometrics not used within continuous authentication systems. Therefore, the demographic bias on some biometrics has been little studied. However, continuous authentication systems that are designed for mainstream use must be aware of the effects of demographic bias than can occur. System designers should consider how data collection, datasets, and training approaches could cause bias due to demographic issues and attempt to minimise potential issues.

5.4 Power Usage

Continuous biometric authentication systems require the sampling and processing of sensor data to fulfil their functionality. This process uses energy that it obtains from the power source of the device. This may not be an issue for mains-powered devices, such as desktop computers, but is an issue for many battery-powered mobile devices such as smartphones, tablets, and smartwatches. It would be detrimental to the usability and transparency of a system if the system resulted in a battery drainage of twice the usual rate. Whilst many continuous biometric authentication systems have aimed to optimise for accuracy, fewer systems have sought to optimise for power usage. This is possibly due to many systems being developed as on devices different to the intended device, such that the real-world power usage is unknown.

There have been some studies that have considered the power usage of the system developed. One study looking at touchscreen gestures includes an analysis of the energy consumption of their system [13]. They found that the power consumption of the system had an average value of 88 mW and did not exceed 6.2% battery usage. Another study created a framework enabling Android developers to create and improve systems incrementally [25]. The study performed the energy consumption analysis utilising *PowerTutor* [45], an application that reports smartphone energy measurements. Through measuring energy consumption of three types of continuous authentication system, the authors found the energy overhead varied between 1.2% and 6.2%. In [38], the authors authenticated grasp, hold, and tap behaviour on smartphones and measured energy consumption with a *Monsoon Power Monitor*. The analysis showed that sensor features extracted at a 16 Hz sensor sampling rate incurred a minor overhead of 7.9% without sacrificing authentication accuracy.

Several studies have investigated and compared various sensors and their power drain. One such study explores a variety of sensors on smartphone devices, including the rotation, accelerometer, GPS, microphone, Wi-Fi, and cellular sensors [28]. They found that the GPS sensor drained the battery the most, with an average battery consumption of 2.31 mAh. They also reported, as would be expected, that increasing the sampling rate decreased the mAh consumed. In [32], the authors explore the potential of a Resource Profile Curve to select an optimal trade-off between authentication accuracy and resource usage. They propose switching between high accuracy but high energy biometrics (such as the face) and low accuracy but low energy biometrics (such as gait) based on the need of the system. The strategy towards reducing energy consumption in [6] selectively turned off motion sensors based on the sensitivity of the current application and the probability the smartphone is given to another user. In cases where the user rarely shared their phone, the approach resulted in a more than 90% energy saving. When designing a continuous biometric authentication system, it is crucial to consider the energy usage to run the desired sensors and computation.

5.5 Attack Mitigation

There are a variety of threats that continuous biometric authentication systems can face. Many of these threats have been described in Sect. 3.8. These threats can be used by impostors to perform an attack that thwarts the authentication process and gains them access to a system that they should not have access to. It is therefore paramount that measures are put into place that mitigates these threats and prevents them being successfully used to attack a system and bypass the authentication process. Some solutions have been proposed for traditional authentication techniques such as shoulder-surfing attacks on knowledge-based authentication [26]. However, mitigating attacks on continuous biometric authentication systems is difficult due to the complexities of the biometrics introducing a variety of attack points [8].

There have been studies proposing attacks on continuous biometric authentication schemes and others proposing mitigation approaches to these attacks. One such study (described in Sect. 3.8) sees a child's Lego toy used to replicate touchscreen gestures performed by human users after gaining access to the processed features [36]. A mitigation for this type of attack was shown in [17]. The study showed that subtle changes in screen settings (a result of a randomised secret) caused identifiable user behaviour change that would not be present in robots. This type of attack, in which spoofed or fake data is presented to a biometric sensor with the intention to interfere with the operation of the system, is a type of *presentation attack*.

In 2015, it was reported that an investor had said that 'either a password or a biometric be stolen, but only the password can be changed. Once your fingerprint is stolen, it's stolen forever, and you're stuck'. However, whilst biometrics may be stolen, unlike a stolen password, biometrics do have a body of research dedicated to checking that the input came from a real human being. This is known as *liveness detection* or *spoof detection*.[2] In the case of the above example, whilst a fingerprint could be stolen, the attacker would have to bypass some liveness detection technology to fool an authentication system that the fingerprint came from a live human. In [41], the authors propose a continuous face-based authentication system for smartphones which extracts LBP and HOG textual features from certain facial regions and classifies them using an SVM as either real or spoofed.

Whilst planning for attack mitigation approaches, it is important to consider not just *uninformed attackers* (which would make up the vast majority of attackers) but also *informed attackers* (which would be more challenging to detect because of their knowledge of the genuine user) [24]. When evaluating the resilience of a continuous biometric authentication scheme against attacks, it is therefore important to consider that there will be informed attackers proactively trying to fool the system with their knowledge. Any attempt to build a continuous biometric authentication system should consider the potential threats and attacks that the system might face and take reasonable measures to mitigate them.

5.6   Privacy

The concept of privacy is defined as the respect and confidentiality of an individual's personal identifying information (PII) or data and the transparent use and storage of it [21]. Often, studies investigating a certain biometric trait do not consider privacy issues as it can go beyond the scope of their research. However, since the development of real-world systems, there has been much interest in providing systems with integrated privacy, despite the *privacy paradox* in which users claim to value privacy but tend to act otherwise [5]. The integration of privacy-preserving techniques requires consideration and should not be done impetuously, because privacy is one of the five key pillars of trustworthy biometric systems[3] [21]. Whilst different systems may require different approaches to integrating privacy, there are several existing solutions that have been proposed to preserve the privacy of biometric data.

Many continuous biometric authentication systems utilise behavioural biometrics, which around 30% of users see as infringing on their privacy [12]. Therefore, it is important that biometric profiles are treated as confidential records. One way of providing this privacy could be provided through the use of *cancellable biometrics* [31], in which biometrics are distorted via a function to the extent that little personal or identifiable information can be obtained from the biometric if stolen. A comparison is done by first using the same distortion function on captured samples. In the event the biometric database is compromised, the distortion function can be

---

[2] These are a type of *presentation attack detection* [35].

[3] The five areas for trustworthy biometrics are (1) Performance Robustness and Scalability, (2) Security, (3) Explainability and Interpretability, (4) Biasness and Fairness, and (5) Privacy [21].

changed, *cancelling* the validity of those in the previous database. A more recent method of ensuring biometric database privacy is *homomorphic encryption* [16]. This is a type of encryption that allows computation to be carried out on encrypted data, such that the biometric profile need not be used in a raw format. However, it has been shown that this approach on fingerprint biometrics may take five times longer [21].

With biometric systems becoming more prevalent within society, there continues to be efforts conducted to build mechanisms that provide privacy. This is not only a key aspect of building trust within the biometric system but in many countries also backed by regulation (see Sect. 5.7). Employing biometrics in a real-world system without proper privacy might lead to attackers obtaining access to the biometric profile or businesses harvesting data for *surveillance capitalism* [47]. Whilst privacy has been out of scope for many continuous biometric authentication studies, there have been some approaches to integrating privacy into these systems [20]. When building a real-world system, privacy should be a crucial consideration.

5.7 Regulatory

In addition to being one of many mechanisms that can authenticate the user identity, biometrics come with the additional concern of being personally identifying information. Unlike a password or a token, biometrics can not only be used as an access mechanism but may also give insight into personal information about a user (such as their race, gender, behaviours, etc.). The improper use/storage of biometric data would therefore erode trust in biometric systems. One of the ways to maintain this trust is through providing privacy of biometric data by ensuring it is treated with respect, confidentiality, and transparency [21]. Violations of such privacy considerations could also have societal implications, which has led to legislation. In 2017 the number of countries that had enacted data privacy laws was 120, with other countries set to follow [18]. Some of these data privacy laws cover biometrics and in some cases can be directly traced to the growth of biometrics (especially the face) [21].

One of the first relevant laws was the Biometric Information Privacy Act (BIPA), passed by the Illinois legislature in 2008 to regulate what private organisations can do with biometric data [1]. Businesses using biometrics in Illinois must (i) inform users that biometrics are collected or stored, (ii) inform users of the purpose and length for which biometrics are collected, stored, and used, (iii) obtain written release from the user to use their biometrics, and (iv) store, transmit, and protect biometrics with a reasonable standard of care. Failure to comply with BIPA can yield penalties of up to $5000 (or actual damages, whichever is greater) for a violation. There have been prominent cases relating to BIPA, including in 2020 where a class action against *Clearview AI* was initiated for their collection of face biometrics [39].

Another prevalent act covering biometrics is the General Data Protection Regulation (GDPR), which was passed by the European Parliament in 2016 and came into effect in May 2018 [10]. The GDPR regulates the processing of categories of personal data, including biometrics. The GDPR sets seven principles, these include lawful, fair and transparent processing, the processing of data explicitly and legitimately, and that data is processed with integrity and confidentiality. There are severe financial penalties for GDPR violation with a maximum fine of €20 million or 4% of global revenue (whichever is higher). Whilst no longer being a member of the EU, the UK maintains regulation on biometric data processing. Since the GDPR, similar legislation has been enacted, such as the California Consumer Privacy Act (CCPA), signed into law in 2018 and effective from 2020, which offers similar protections on personal data (including biometrics) with financial penalties for violations.

The increased use of biometrics over the last several decades has clearly motivated some of the data privacy laws. However, whilst some countries have stringent laws surrounding the use of biometrics, it must be noted that data privacy laws are different in different countries [18]. When deploying a continuous biometric authentication system, it is therefore crucial that the system is built in accordance with local laws. It is not only beneficial from a legal standpoint but can also increase trust in the biometric system if it is implemented with data privacy considerations [21].

5.8   Drift

As discussed in Sect. 4.2, one desirable requirement for optimal biometric traits is that of permanence. However, in practice, many biometrics that have been discussed do, at different paces, change over time. Some of these changes are due to physiological changes (e.g., facial aging or beard growth), whereas others can be due to behavioural adaptation (e.g., as users become better at a specific task). However, many of the continuous biometric authentication systems that have been discussed have been short-term studies that have constructed user profiles with biometrics and tested the system on biometrics collected soon after. Therefore, some systems have not explored the effects of significant time between training and test samples. With most biometrics, as the time between the training and test samples increases, so would the FRR. This drift from the biometric profile is a type of *concept drift* [46], referring to the drift of new data away from an initially accurate profile.

In the *Touchalytics* study [14], the authors investigated continuous touchscreen gesture authentication on smartphones. They reported that in an inter-week authentication approach the horizontal scrolls saw a higher fraction of falsely rejected gestures, implying possible concept drift. In [7], a Kernel Deep Regression Network (KDRN) is used to authenticate touchscreen gestures. They reported an EER of 0.013% for intra-session authentication, 0.023% for inter-session authentication, and 0.121% for inter-week authentication. This also sees potential signs of concept drift. Given the flexible nature of behavioural traits, a solution in [27] uses a dynamic profile technique in which profiles contained 7, 10, or 14 days of user's most recent activities that was updated on a daily basis. The downside of this type of approach is that, without careful analysis, it may be possible for attackers to gradually poison the profile [22]. Further investigation is needed, but few biometric datasets cover a sufficiently large period of time to facilitate this research.

The problem of concept drift within the biometric domain has seen efforts to mitigate drift in real-world biometric authentication solutions. The face authentication solution on some Apple iPhone devices apparently augments its stored mathematical representation over time [2]. Their approach may store a successfully authenticated representation of a face, if it is of sufficient quality, for a number of additional authentication attempts before the data is discarded. The approach will also capture a face and temporarily augment the stored facial representation if a prior face is not authenticated but is above a certain threshold and followed by the correct passcode. These approaches allow a robust and dynamic profile that is not restricted solely to the original representation of the user when they enrolled. Whilst such solutions for concept drift within continuous biometric authentication systems are not widespread, they are an important consideration for a solution with longevity.

5.9 Summary

This chapter has outlined a variety of considerations and challenges that should be given thought as part of the journey towards forming a continuous biometric authentication system. There are multiple considerations applicable to such systems. These include contextual awareness, attack mitigation strategies, and privacy-preserving biometric comparisons. When building continuous biometric authentication systems for real-world use, it is important to address the considerations and challenges such a system faces. Addressing them has benefits not only to the operation of the system but also to the trust a user would have in the system.

References

1. (2008). https://www.ilga.gov/legislation/ilcs/ilcs3.asp?ActID=3004&ChapterID=57
2. (2021). https://manuals.info.apple.com/MANUALS/1000/MA1902/en_US/apple-platform-security-guide.pdf
3. Abowd, G.D., Dey, A.K., Brown, P.J., Davies, N., Smith, M., Steggles, P.: Towards a better understanding of context and context-awareness. In: Gellersen, H.W. (ed.) Handheld and Ubiquitous Computing, pp. 304–307. Springer Berlin Heidelberg, Berlin (1999)
4. Ahmed, M.: UK passport photo checker shows bias against dark-skinned women (2020). https://www.bbc.co.uk/news/technology-54349538
5. Anderson, R.J.: Security Engineering: A Guide to Building Dependable Distributed Systems, 3 edn. Wiley Publishing, New York (2021)

6. Bo, C., Zhang, L., Li, X.Y., Huang, Q., Wang, Y.: SilentSense: silent user identification via touch and movement behavioral biometrics. In: Proceedings of the 19th International Conference on Mobile Computing & Networking, pp. 187–190 (2013)
7. Chang, I., Low, C.Y., Choi, S., Teoh, A.B.J.: Kernel deep regression network for touch-stroke dynamics authentication. IEEE Signal Process Lett. 25(7), 1109–1113 (2018)
8. Clarke, N.: Transparent User Authentication: Biometrics, RFID and Behavioural Profiling, 1st edn. Springer Publishing Company, Inc., Berlin (2011)
9. Crawford, H., Ahmadzadeh, E.: Authentication on the go: assessing the effect of movement on mobile device keystroke dynamics. In: Thirteenth Symposium on Usable Privacy and Security (SOUPS 2017), pp. 163–173. USENIX Association, Santa Clara (2017)
10. De Silva, S., Liu, A., LLP, N.: Europe's tough new law on biometrics. Biom. Technol. Today 2017(2), 5–7 (2017)
11. Drozdowski, P., Rathgeb, C., Dantcheva, A., Damer, N., Busch, C.: Demographic bias in biometrics: A survey on an emerging challenge. IEEE Trans. Technol. Soc. 1(2), 89–103 (2020)
12. Earl, S., Campbell, J., Buckley, O.: Investigating what you share: privacy perceptions of behavioural biometrics. In: Stephanidis, C., Antona, M., Ntoa, S. (eds.) HCI International 2021—Posters, pp. 408–415. Springer International Publishing, Cham (2021)
13. Feng, T., Yang, J., Yan, Z., Tapia, E.M., Shi, W.: Tips: context-aware implicit user identification using touch screen in uncontrolled environments. In: Proceedings of the 15th Workshop on Mobile Computing Systems and Applications, HotMobile '14. Association for Computing Machinery, New York (2014)
14. Frank, M., Biedert, R., Ma, E., Martinovic, I., Song, D.: Touchalytics: on the applicability of touchscreen input as a behavioral biometric for continuous authentication. IEEE Trans. Inf. Forensics Secur. 8(1), 136–148 (2013)
15. Galton, F.: Personal identification and description. Nature 38(973), 173–177 (1888)
16. Gomez-Barrero, M., Maiorana, E., Galbally, J., Campisi, P., Fierrez, J.: Multi-biometric template protection based on homomorphic encryption. Pattern Recogn. 67, 149–163 (2017)
17. Gong, N.Z., Payer, M., Moazzezi, R., Frank, M.: Forgery-resistant touch-based authentication on mobile devices. In: Proceedings of the 11th ACM on Asia Conference on Computer and Communications Security, ASIA CCS '16, pp. 499–510. Association for Computing Machinery, New York (2016)
18. Greenleaf, G.: Global data privacy laws 2017: 120 national data privacy laws, including Indonesia and Turkey. In: 145 Privacy Laws & Business International Report, pp. 10–13 (2017)
19. Grother, P., Ngan, M., Hanaoka, K.: Face recognition vendor test part 3: demographic effects (2019). https://doi.org/10.6028/NIST.IR.8280
20. Hernández-Álvarez, L., de Fuentes, J.M., González-Manzano, L., Hernández Encinas, L.: Privacy-preserving sensor-based continuous authentication and user profiling: A review. Sensors 21(1), 92 (2021)
21. Jain, A.K., Deb, D., Engelsma, J.J.: Biometrics: trust, but verify. CoRR abs/2105.06625 (2021)
22. Kantchelian, A., Afroz, S., Huang, L., Islam, A.C., Miller, B., Tschantz, M.C., Greenstadt, R., Joseph, A.D., Tygar, J.: Approaches to adversarial drift. In: Proceedings of the 2013 ACM Workshop on Artificial Intelligence and Security, pp. 99–110 (2013)
23. Karkkainen, K., Joo, J.: FairFace: face attribute dataset for balanced race, gender, and age for bias measurement and mitigation. In: Proceedings of the IEEE/CVF Winter Conference on Applications of Computer Vision (WACV), pp. 1548–1558 (2021)
24. Kayacik, H.G., Just, M., Baillie, L., Aspinall, D., Micallef, N.: Data driven authentication: on the effectiveness of user behaviour modelling with mobile device sensors. arXiv preprint arXiv:1410.7743 (2014)
25. Khan, H., Atwater, A., Hengartner, U.: ITUs: An implicit authentication framework for android. In: Proceedings of the 20th Annual International Conference on Mobile Computing and Networking, MobiCom '14, pp. 507–518. Association for Computing Machinery, New York (2014)
26. Lee, M.K.: Security notions and advanced method for human shoulder-surfing resistant pin-entry. IEEE Trans. Inf. Forensics Secur. 9(4), 695–708 (2014)

27. Li, F., Clarke, N., Papadaki, M., Dowland, P.: Active authentication for mobile devices utilising behaviour profiling. Int. J. Inf. Secur. **13**, 229–244 (2014)
28. Micallef, N., Kayacık, H.G., Just, M., Baillie, L., Aspinall, D.: Sensor use and usefulness: trade-offs for data-driven authentication on mobile devices. In: 2015 IEEE International Conference on Pervasive Computing and Communications (PerCom), pp. 189–197 (2015)
29. Mondal, S., Bours, P.: Does context matter for the performance of continuous authentication biometric systems? an empirical study on mobile device. In: 2015 International Conference of the Biometrics Special Interest Group (BIOSIG), pp. 1–5 (2015)
30. Patel, V.M., Chellappa, R., Chandra, D., Barbello, B.: Continuous user authentication on mobile devices: recent progress and remaining challenges. IEEE Signal Process. Mag. **33**(4), 49–61 (2016)
31. Patel, V.M., Ratha, N.K., Chellappa, R.: Cancelable biometrics: A review. IEEE Signal Process. Mag. **32**(5), 54–65 (2015)
32. Rasnayaka, S., Saha, S., Sim, T.: Making the most of what you have! profiling biometric authentication on mobile devices. In: 2019 International Conference on Biometrics (ICB), pp. 1–7 (2019)
33. Rathgeb, C., Drozdowski, P., Damer, N., Frings, D.C., Busch, C.: Demographic Fairness in Biometric Systems: What do the Experts Say? (2021)
34. Samangouei, P., Patel, V.M., Chellappa, R.: Facial attributes for active authentication on mobile devices. Image Vision Comput. **58**, 181–192 (2017)
35. Schuckers, S.: Presentations and attacks, and spoofs, oh my. Image Vis. Comput. **55**, 26–30 (2016). Recognizing future hot topics and hard problems in biometrics research
36. Serwadda, A., Phoha, V.V., Wang, Z., Kumar, R., Shukla, D.: Toward robotic robbery on the touch screen. ACM Trans. Inf. Syst. Secur. **18**(4), 1–25 (2016)
37. Siirtola, P., Komulainen, J., Kellokumpu, V.: Effect of context in swipe gesture-based continuous authentication on smartphones. In: 26th European Symposium on Artificial Neural Networks, ESANN 2018, Bruges, Belgium, April 25–27, 2018 (2018)
38. Sitová, Z., Šeděnka, J., Yang, Q., Peng, G., Zhou, G., Gasti, P., Balagani, K.S.: HMOG: new behavioral biometric features for continuous authentication of smartphone users. IEEE Trans. Inf. Forensics Secur. **11**(5), 877–892 (2016)
39. Smith, M., Miller, S.: The ethical application of biometric facial recognition technology. AI & SOCIETY (2021)
40. Smith-Creasey, M., Albalooshi, F.A., Rajarajan, M.: Context awareness for improved continuous face authentication on mobile devices. In: 2018 IEEE 16th International Conference on Dependable, Autonomic and Secure Computing, 16th International Conference on Pervasive Intelligence and Computing, 4th International Conference on Big Data Intelligence and Computing and Cyber Science and Technology Congress(DASC/PiCom/DataCom/CyberSciTech), pp. 644–652 (2018)
41. Smith-Creasey, M., Albalooshi, F.A., Rajarajan, M.: Continuous face authentication scheme for mobile devices with tracking and liveness detection. Microprocess. Microsyst. **63**, 147–157 (2018)
42. Smith-Creasey, M., Rajarajan, M.: A novel word-independent gesture-typing continuous authentication scheme for mobile devices. Comput. Secur. **83**, 140–150 (2019)
43. Terhörst, P., Fährmann, D., Damer, N., Kirchbuchner, F., Kuijper, A.: On soft-biometric information stored in biometric face embeddings. IEEE Trans. Biom. Behav. Identity Sci. **3**(4), 519–534 (2021)
44. Young, S.G., Hugenberg, K., Bernstein, M.J., Sacco, D.F.: Perception and motivation in face recognition: A critical review of theories of the cross-race effect. Personal. Soc. Psychol. Rev. **16**(2), 116–142 (2012)
45. Zhang, L., Tiwana, B., Qian, Z., Wang, Z., Dick, R.P., Mao, Z.M., Yang, L.: Accurate online power estimation and automatic battery behavior based power model generation for smartphones. In: Proceedings of the Eighth IEEE/ACM/IFIP International Conference on Hardware/Software Codesign and System Synthesis, CODES/ISSS '10, pp. 105–114. Association for Computing Machinery, New York (2010)

46. Žliobaitė, I., Pechenizkiy, M., Gama, J.: An overview of concept drift applications. In: Big Data Analysis: New Algorithms for a New Society, pp. 91–114 (2016)
47. Zuboff, S.: Surveillance capitalism and the challenge of collective action. New Labor Forum **28**(1), 10–29 (2019)

Chapter 6
Conclusion

6.1 Summary

Most users authenticate today via traditional authentication techniques. These techniques fit into three different categories: (1) something you *know*, (2) something you *have*, and (3) something you *are*. Many systems today still use passwords, which often result in users fighting security for usability by selecting memorable but weak passwords. These traditional techniques are often implemented solely at the point of entry, meaning that once a system is unlocked an attacker may be able to obtain access. There is also research indicating that traditional techniques are often seen as inconvenient. This motivates the need for continuous authentication.

The concept of a continuous biometric authentication system is one that collects biometrics continuously (or frequently) during usage, such that they can be matched against a user profile to enforce an access policy. These systems can be implemented on a variety of different devices, utilising a variety of different biometrics. Some systems employ multiple biometrics. These systems generally have a positive reception from users that have trialled or been surveyed about such solutions.

The area of biometrics is a mature research field with many different modalities studied. There are some requirements of optimal biometrics that can help with selecting modalities, including permanence, distinctiveness, universality, and more. There are two key groups of biometrics, namely physiological and behavioural. There are a variety of different modalities that have been implemented (sometimes together) within continuous biometric authentication systems.

There are some considerations that must be addressed when implementing a continuous biometric authentication system for real-world use. These include factoring in contextual awareness, power usage, attack mitigation, and privacy concerns. These considerations also present research challenges since many current solutions to address them indicate there is still work to be done. Through factoring in such considerations, it is likely to improve system performance and user trust.

M. Smith-Creasey, *Continuous Biometric Authentication Systems*, SpringerBriefs in Computer Science, https://doi.org/10.1007/978-3-031-49071-2_6

6.2   Further Reading

This section will briefly note some works that have been important in the development of continuous biometric authentication systems.

- Jain, A.K., Ross, A.A., Nandakumar, K., 2011. *Introduction to biometrics*. Springer US.
- Clarke, N., 2011. *Transparent user authentication: biometrics, RFID and behavioural profiling*. Springer Science & Business Media.
- Ross, A.A., Nandakumar, K. and Jain, A.K., 2006. *Handbook of multibiometrics*. Springer Science & Business Media.

6.3   Notes

Thank you for taking the time to read *Continuous Biometric Authentication Systems*. Please note the following. This book has been written solely by Max Smith-Creasey. The book presents an overview of existing literature, any novel contributions described within are those of the authors cited. Every effort has gone into ensuring accuracy, any mistakes are unintentional, and the author is not liable for any consequences that arise from this. If informed of errata, the author will be happy to attempt amending the issue in any future versions. The book was produced based on an agreement only between Springer and the author. The book is not affiliated with the author's employers (past or present) and should not be seen as a reflection of their views or intentions on the subject.

Printed in the United States
by Baker & Taylor Publisher Services